AMAZING COINCIDENCES

100 Events That Defy Explanation

Copper Moon Press

Table of Contents

Introduction

In a world governed by the laws of probability and chance, there exist moments that seem to defy explanation – instances where the improbable becomes reality, and the impossible manifests before our eyes. These are the stories that make us question the very fabric of our existence, that spark wonder and awe in even the most skeptical minds.

"**AMAZING COINCIDENCES**" is a collection of one hundred true tales that challenge our understanding of chance and fate. From the eerily prophetic dreams that saved lives to the inexplicable connections between strangers across time and space, each story in this book invites us to ponder the mysterious forces that shape our world.

Within these pages, you'll encounter twin brothers reunited by a car crash, a parrot whose squawks predicted an earthquake, and a man whose tattoo won him the lottery. You'll read about time-traveling postcards, reincarnated artists, and scientific discoveries made simultaneously on opposite sides of the globe. These aren't works of fiction or flights of fancy – they are documented events that have left witnesses and experts alike searching for explanations.

As you delve into these extraordinary accounts, you may find yourself questioning the nature of reality, the limits of human intuition, and the possibility of unseen connections binding us all. Are these events merely the product of chance, amplified by our human tendency to seek patterns and meaning? Or do they point to a deeper order in the universe, a hidden design that occasionally reveals itself through these astonishing coincidences?

"**AMAZING COINCIDENCES**" doesn't claim to have all the answers. Instead, it invites you on a journey through the improbable and the extraordinary, encouraging you to keep an open mind and to embrace the wonder of the unexplained. In a world that often seems chaotic and random, these stories remind us that magic and mystery still exist – if only we're willing to see it.

Prepare to be amazed, perplexed, and inspired as you explore the thin line between chance and destiny in "**AMAZING COINCIDENCES: 100 Events That Defy Explanation.**"

Chapter One

The Curious Case of the Time-Traveling Telegram

In the annals of peculiar coincidences, few stories are as intriguing as the case of the time-traveling telegram that arrived in Waco, Texas, in 1950. This extraordinary event blurred the lines between past and present, leaving those involved scratching their heads in disbelief.

On a seemingly ordinary day in 1950, Waco resident Clyde Ballard received a most unexpected delivery. A Western Union messenger handed him a telegram, a common enough occurrence in those days. However, upon opening it, Ballard was astonished to find that the message had been sent 75 years earlier, in 1875.

The telegram had been dispatched by a cattle buyer named Renus Barrett, who had sent it from Brownsville, Texas, to his business partner in Waco. Its contents were simple enough - a request for $100 to be sent immediately for a cattle purchase. But the real story wasn't in the message itself, but in its incredible journey through time.

For three-quarters of a century, this small piece of paper had been lost in the labyrinthine system of telegraph offices, somehow evading detection and delivery. It had survived wars, economic depressions, and the rapid technological changes that had transformed America from a frontier nation to a modern superpower.

When the telegram finally emerged from its temporal limbo, it caused quite a stir. Western Union officials were baffled, unable to explain how the message had remained undelivered for so long. Historians were thrilled, viewing the telegram as a tangible link to the Old West era.

For Clyde Ballard, the recipient, it was a surreal experience. He had no connection to either the sender or the intended recipient, both of whom had long since passed away. Yet here he was, holding a piece of their long-forgotten correspondence.

The story of the time-traveling telegram quickly spread, capturing imaginations across the country. It served as a reminder of the unpredictable nature of life and the strange ways in which the past can sometimes reach out and touch the present.

To this day, the case of the 75-year-delayed telegram remains one of the most curious examples of coincidence in American postal history. It stands as a testament to the enduring power of written communication and the mysterious workings of chance and time.

Chapter Two

The Uncanny Parallels Between Lincoln and Kennedy

In the annals of American history, few coincidences are as striking as the parallels between two of the nation's most beloved presidents: Abraham Lincoln and John F. Kennedy. Despite being separated by a century, the lives and deaths of these two men share an astonishing number of similarities that have captivated the public imagination for decades.

Both Lincoln and Kennedy were elected to Congress in '46 - 1846 and 1946, respectively. Each man then ascended to the presidency in '60 - Lincoln in 1860 and Kennedy in 1960. This temporal symmetry is just the beginning of their shared narrative.

Perhaps the most chilling parallel lies in their assassinations. Both presidents were shot on a Friday, and more specifically, each was shot in the head while seated beside his wife. The tragedy of their deaths was compounded by the fact that both were killed in the presence of another couple.

The similarities extend to their assassins as well. John Wilkes Booth and Lee Harvey Oswald were both Southerners with three names, each containing 15 letters. Both were killed before they could be brought to trial, adding an element of mystery to each assassination that persists to this day.

In the aftermath of these tragedies, both presidents were succeeded by men named Johnson. Andrew Johnson, who followed Lincoln, was born in 1808. A century later, in 1908, Lyndon B. Johnson was born. This cosmic symmetry in their successors' births adds another layer to the already remarkable coincidences.

While skeptics argue that such parallels can be found between any two historical figures if one looks hard enough, the sheer number and specificity of the Lincoln-Kennedy connections continue to intrigue many. These coincidences have spawned numerous books, articles, and discussions, becoming a part of American folklore.

Whether viewed as mere chance or something more mysterious, the Lincoln-Kennedy parallels serve as a reminder of the unpredictable nature of history and the strange ways in which patterns can emerge across time. They continue to fascinate us, inviting contemplation on the intricate tapestry of American presidential history.

Chapter Three

Twin Brothers' Parallel Deaths: A Tale of Uncanny Synchronicity

In 2002, the world witnessed one of the most extraordinary examples of twin synchronicity ever recorded. Two 70-year-old identical twin brothers, whose lives had been intertwined since conception, died on the same day, within hours of each other, in different locations. What makes this story even more remarkable is that neither twin was aware of the other's passing.

The brothers, whose names were withheld for privacy reasons, had lived in separate towns in northern Finland. Despite the physical distance between them, they had maintained a close relationship throughout their lives, sharing the deep bond that often exists between identical twins.

On a seemingly ordinary day in March 2002, the first twin was riding his bicycle along a busy road in Raahe, a town on Finland's northwest coast. In a tragic turn of events, he was struck by a lorry and killed instantly. The accident sent shockwaves through the local community, but little did anyone know that this was only half of an incredible cosmic coincidence.

Just two hours later and 600 kilometers away, the second twin was crossing a road in Helenelund, just north of Stockholm, Sweden. In a chilling echo of his brother's fate, he too was hit by a truck and died at the scene. The chances of such identical accidents occurring to twins on the same day are astronomically small, leading many to wonder about the nature of the connection between twins.

News of this extraordinary coincidence spread quickly, captivating people around the world. Scientists and twin researchers were particularly intrigued, seeing it as a potential case study in the mysterious bond between identical twins. Some speculated about the possibility of a shared genetic predisposition to certain types of accidents, while others pondered more esoteric explanations involving twin telepathy or shared consciousness.

For the families of the brothers, the simultaneous loss was both devastating and awe-inspiring. While grappling with their grief, they couldn't help but marvel at the synchronized nature of the twins' departures from this world. It seemed as if, even in death, the brothers couldn't bear to be apart.

This remarkable story serves as a poignant reminder of the deep connections that can exist between twins and the unpredictable nature of life and death. It continues to fascinate those interested in twin studies, coincidences, and the mysteries of human existence.

Chapter Four

The Falling Baby Miracle: Joseph Figlock's Incredible Catches

In the realm of improbable events, the story of Joseph Figlock and baby Etta Ng stands out as truly extraordinary. This tale of miraculous saves, which unfolded in Detroit in the late 1930s, seems to defy the laws of probability and has since become a celebrated example of incredible coincidence.

Joseph Figlock was a street sweeper in Detroit, going about his daily routine of keeping the city clean. Little did he know that his job was about to intersect with destiny in the most unexpected way. In 1937, as Figlock was sweeping near an apartment building, his life changed in an instant.

From a fourth-floor window of the building, a baby named Etta Ng suddenly fell. In a heart-stopping moment, the infant plummeted towards the hard pavement below. But fate had other plans. Joseph Figlock, in the right place at the precisely right time, inadvertently caught the falling baby. Both Figlock and Etta were shaken but unharmed, and what could have been a tragedy became a miracle.

This event alone would be remarkable enough to be remembered for years. However, the story doesn't end there. In a twist that seems almost too incredible to be true, history repeated itself a year later.

In 1938, Figlock was once again sweeping the streets near the same apartment building. Incredibly, the same baby, Etta Ng, fell from the same fourth-floor window. And once again, Joseph Figlock was there to break her fall. For the second time, both the baby and her accidental savior escaped serious injury.

The odds of such an event happening once are astronomical. The probability of it occurring twice, with the same individuals involved, is beyond calculation. This double miracle captivated the public imagination, making headlines across the country and cementing Figlock's status as an unwitting hero.

This extraordinary coincidence raises questions about fate, luck, and the mysterious workings of the universe. Was it mere chance, or was there some greater force at work? The story of Joseph Figlock and Etta Ng continues to be retold, a testament to the unpredictable and sometimes miraculous nature of life.

Last edited 55 minutes ago

Chapter Five

Separated Twins' Mirrored Lives: The Uncanny Tale of Jim Lewis and Jim Springer

The story of Jim Lewis and Jim Springer is a testament to the power of genetics and the mysterious connections that can exist between twins, even when separated at birth. Their tale, which unfolded in the late 20th century, is one of the most striking examples of coincidence in the annals of twin studies.

Born in 1940, the identical twins were put up for adoption and separated at just four weeks old. They grew up 45 miles apart in Ohio, each unaware of the other's existence. It wasn't until 1979, at the age of 39, that they finally reunited, setting the stage for a series of astonishing discoveries about their parallel lives.

The coincidences began with their names. Both had been named James by their respective adoptive parents, and both went by Jim. But this was just the tip of the iceberg. As they shared their life stories, the similarities piled up in ways that seemed to defy mere chance.

Both Jims had married women named Linda, divorced, and then re-married women named Betty. They both had sons – one named James Alan and the other named James Allan. Both had childhood dogs named Toy. The coincidences extended to their habits and hobbies too. Both chain-smoked the same brand of cigarettes, enjoyed ice-cold beer, and had woodworking shops in their garages.

Their career paths also showed remarkable similarities. Both had worked part-time in law enforcement as sheriffs in different Ohio counties. They both enjoyed mechanical drawing and carpentry. Even their vacations aligned – both families had driven to the same beach in Florida for family getaways, though at different times.

The case of the Jim twins, as they came to be known, became a sensation in the world of psychology and genetics. Researchers saw it as a unique opportunity to study the effects of nature versus nurture. The extent of their similarities, despite growing up in separate environments, suggested a strong genetic influence on personality and behavior.

Their story challenges our understanding of individuality and the forces that shape our lives. It raises profound questions about free will and determinism, and the complex interplay between our genes and our environments. The Jim twins' mirrored lives continue to fascinate scientists and the public alike, serving as a remarkable example of life's unpredictable symmetries.

Chapter Six

The Titanic Premonition: Morgan Robertson's Eerie Prediction

In the annals of literary prophecy, few stories are as chilling and precise as Morgan Robertson's novella "Futility, or the Wreck of the Titan." Published in 1898, a full 14 years before the tragic sinking of the RMS Titanic, Robertson's tale bore such striking similarities to the real-life disaster that it has since been hailed as one of the most remarkable premonitions in history.

Robertson's novella tells the story of a supposedly unsinkable ocean liner named Titan. This fictional ship, like its real-life counterpart, was one of the largest vessels of its time. The Titan, described as the largest craft afloat and the greatest of the works of men, bore an uncanny resemblance to the Titanic in both its features and its fate.

The similarities between fiction and reality are nothing short of astonishing. Both ships were triple-screw vessels about 800 feet long, capable of carrying about 3,000 people. Both were described as "unsinkable" and both carried too few lifeboats for the number of people on board. In Robertson's tale, the Titan hit an iceberg in the North Atlantic in April, sinking with a huge loss of life – a scenario that played out with eerie accuracy when the Titanic met its doom in April 1912.

Even more remarkably, both ships were traveling at similar speeds (25 knots in the book, 22.5 knots in reality) when they struck an iceberg on the starboard side. Both sank about 400 miles from Newfoundland, and both events resulted in the deaths of more than half of their passengers and crew.

The parallels between Robertson's fiction and the Titanic disaster are so numerous and specific that they seem to defy coincidence. This has led many to speculate about the nature of Robertson's "prediction." Was it merely an uncanny guess, or did Robertson possess some sort of precognitive ability?

Skeptics argue that Robertson, as a experienced seaman and writer, simply combined his knowledge of maritime trends with creative speculation. They point out that the idea of a luxurious, "unsinkable" ship was already in the zeitgeist of the late 19th century.

Regardless of how one interprets it, the story of "Futility" remains one of the most famous examples of apparent precognition in literature. It serves as a haunting reminder of the thin line between fiction and reality, and the mysterious ways in which art can sometimes seem to predict life.

Chapter Seven

Mark Twain and Halley's Comet: A Cosmic Coincidence

The life of Samuel Clemens, better known by his pen name Mark Twain, was bookended by one of the most spectacular celestial events visible from Earth – the appearance of Halley's Comet. This cosmic coincidence, spanning the great American author's entire life, has become one of the most famous examples of prophetic wit in literary history.

Mark Twain was born on November 30, 1835, two weeks after the perihelion of Halley's Comet. The comet, which appears in Earth's skies approximately every 75 years, had made its closest approach to the sun on November 16, creating a spectacular sight in the night sky. Little did anyone know that the baby born in that comet's glow would grow up to become one of America's most beloved authors.

Throughout his life, Twain was aware of this cosmic connection and often joked about it. In 1909, when he was 74 years old, he made a famous prediction about his own death. He said, "I came in with Halley's Comet in 1835. It is coming again next year, and I expect to go out with it. It will be the greatest disappointment of my life if I don't go out with Halley's Comet. The Almighty has said, no doubt: 'Now here are these two unaccountable freaks; they came in together, they must go out together.'"

True to his prediction, Twain died on April 21, 1910, just one day after Halley's Comet reached its perihelion. The comet, visible to the naked eye at the time, seemed to have come to escort the great writer on his final journey. Twain's death, perfectly timed with the comet's return, turned his humorous prediction into a self-fulfilling prophecy.

This remarkable coincidence has since become an integral part of Twain's legend. It speaks to his larger-than-life personality and his knack for memorable quips. More than that, it seems to suggest a cosmic poetry to Twain's life – a sense that his existence was somehow aligned with the grand movements of the universe.

The story of Twain and Halley's Comet continues to captivate people today. It serves as a poignant reminder of the cyclical nature of life and the universe, and the strange synchronicities that can occur when human lives intersect with cosmic events. In this way, Twain's connection to the comet has become a fitting metaphor for his enduring place in the literary firmament.

Chapter Eight

The Revenge of Timur's Tomb: A Historical Coincidence

In the annals of archaeological discoveries, few stories are as chilling and seemingly prophetic as the opening of Timur's tomb in 1941. Timur, also known as Tamerlane, was a fearsome Turko-Mongol conqueror who ruled over an empire stretching from India to Turkey in the 14th century. His final resting place in Samarkand, Uzbekistan, had remained undisturbed for centuries until a team of Soviet archaeologists decided to exhume his body.

The expedition was led by Mikhail Gerasimov, a renowned Soviet anthropologist. Despite warnings from local elders and religious leaders about a curse supposedly protecting the tomb, the team proceeded with their plans. An inscription on Timur's casket ominously read, "Whoever opens my tomb shall unleash an invader more terrible than I." These words would prove to be eerily prophetic.

On June 20, 1941, Gerasimov's team opened the tomb and exhumed Timur's remains. The corpse was found to be well-preserved, and the scientists began their examinations. However, their academic curiosity was soon overshadowed by world events of cataclysmic proportions.

Just two days later, on June 22, 1941, Nazi Germany launched Operation Barbarossa, a massive invasion of the Soviet Union. This attack, involving

15

over three million Axis soldiers, caught the Soviets off guard and became one of the largest and deadliest military operations in history.

The timing of these events - the tomb's opening followed so closely by the invasion - struck many as more than mere coincidence. It seemed as if Timur's curse had come to life, with Hitler playing the role of the "invader more terrible" than Timur himself.

The story takes another twist in November 1942. As the Battle of Stalingrad raged, Stalin ordered Timur's remains to be reinterred with full Islamic burial rites. Shortly after this reburial, the Soviet forces launched Operation Uranus, a massive counteroffensive that encircled the German Sixth Army and marked a turning point in the war.

Whether viewed as coincidence or something more mysterious, the tale of Timur's tomb has become a part of World War II folklore. It serves as a reminder of the unpredictable nature of history and the power of ancient legends to captivate our imaginations. The story continues to fascinate historians and the public alike, blending archaeology, superstition, and the grand sweep of 20th-century history into a narrative that seems almost too incredible to be true.

Last edited 51 minutes ago

Chapter Nine

The Erdős-Selfridge Coincidence: A Mathematical Serendipity

In the world of mathematics, coincidences are often viewed with a mixture of skepticism and fascination. However, the story of Paul Erdős and John Selfridge's identical ties stands out as a charming example of serendipity in the lives of two brilliant mathematicians.

Paul Erdős, a Hungarian mathematician, was renowned for his eccentricities as much as for his mathematical genius. He was a prolific collaborator, working with hundreds of mathematicians throughout his career. John Selfridge, an American mathematician, was known for his work in number theory and was one of Erdős's frequent collaborators.

The incident occurred at a mathematics conference where both Erdős and Selfridge were in attendance. As they met, they were surprised to discover that they were wearing exactly the same tie. This might not seem particularly remarkable at first glance - after all, how many variations of ties can there be? However, the coincidence deepens when we consider the circumstances.

Upon discussing their identical neckwear, Erdős and Selfridge realized that they had independently purchased these ties at the same shop, in different cities, on the same day. The probability of such an occurrence is vanishingly small, especially considering the vast number of tie designs and shops available.

For two mathematicians, who spend their lives calculating probabilities and analyzing patterns, this coincidence was particularly delightful. It provided a real-world example of the kind of unlikely events that they often dealt with in abstract terms.

The Erdős-Selfridge tie incident became a favorite anecdote in mathematical circles, often recounted as an example of how even the most rational and logical minds can be surprised by the randomness of the universe. It served as a reminder that coincidences can happen to anyone, anywhere, regardless of their profession or background.

This story also highlights the human side of mathematics. Often perceived as a dry, abstract field, mathematics is full of colorful characters and unexpected moments of humor and coincidence. The tie incident humanizes these brilliant minds, showing that even as they grappled with complex theorems and proofs, they could still be amused and amazed by the simple coincidences of everyday life.

The Erdős-Selfridge coincidence remains a cherished part of mathematical folklore. It stands as a testament to the unpredictable nature of life and the joy that can be found in recognizing and appreciating these moments of serendipity, even (or especially) in the most logical of disciplines.

Chapter Ten

The Booth-Lincoln Connection: A Historical Irony

The assassination of Abraham Lincoln by John Wilkes Booth is one of the most infamous events in American history. However, a lesser-known story connects the Booth family to the Lincolns in a way that seems almost too coincidental to be true. This tale involves Edwin Booth, the brother of John Wilkes Booth, and Robert Todd Lincoln, the son of Abraham Lincoln.

Edwin Booth was a renowned actor, considered by many to be the greatest of his generation. Unlike his brother John, Edwin was a Unionist and supporter of President Lincoln. The incident that forever linked him to the Lincoln family occurred in 1864, approximately a year before the assassination of Abraham Lincoln.

Robert Todd Lincoln, then a young man of 21, was waiting on a crowded train platform in Jersey City, New Jersey. As the train approached, the crowd surged forward, causing Robert to lose his footing. He fell into the gap between the platform and the train, a potentially fatal situation.

At that moment, a man reached out and grabbed Robert by the collar, pulling him to safety. The young Lincoln turned to thank his savior and recognized him as Edwin Booth, whose face was familiar to him from the stage.

Robert Todd Lincoln later recounted this incident in a letter to the editor of The Century Magazine in 1909. He wrote, "The incident occurred while a group of passengers were late at night purchasing their sleeping car places from the conductor who stood on the station platform at the entrance of the car. The platform was about the height of the car floor, and there was of course a narrow space between the platform and the car body. There was some crowding, and I happened to be pressed by it against the car body while waiting my turn. In this situation the train began to move, and by the motion I was twisted off my feet, and had dropped somewhat, with feet downward, into the open space, and was personally helpless, when my coat collar was vigorously seized and I was quickly pulled up and out to a secure footing on the platform. Upon turning to thank my rescuer I saw it was Edwin Booth, whose face was of course well known to me, and I expressed my gratitude to him, and in doing so, called him by name."

Ironically, Edwin Booth did not learn the identity of the young man he had saved until after his brother had assassinated President Lincoln. When he discovered that he had saved the life of Abraham Lincoln's son, it provided him with some solace during a time when he was deeply distressed by his brother's actions.

This remarkable coincidence serves as a poignant footnote to one of the most tragic events in American history. It highlights the complex web of connections that can exist between historical figures and reminds us of the unpredictable nature of human interactions. The Booth-Lincoln connection stands as a testament to the idea that even in the darkest of times, moments of heroism and coincidence can emerge to captivate our historical imagination.

Chapter Eleven

The Ferrari Curse: James Dean's Fateful Porsche

The story of James Dean's "cursed" Porsche 550 Spyder is a tale that blends Hollywood glamour with eerie premonition. It's a narrative that has captivated car enthusiasts and movie fans for decades, centered around one of the most iconic actors of the 1950s and his fateful encounter with a legendary British actor.

In September 1955, James Dean, the rising star of American cinema, purchased a Porsche 550 Spyder. He had recently finished filming "Giant" and was looking forward to pursuing his passion for auto racing. The sleek, silver Porsche was a prized possession for Dean, who nicknamed it "Little Bastard."

On September 23, 1955, Dean was at a service station on Ventura Boulevard in Los Angeles, preparing for a race. It was here that he had a chance encounter with British actor Alec Guinness, already a respected figure in the film industry. Guinness later recounted the meeting in his autobiography.

According to Guinness, Dean proudly showed off his new Porsche. However, Guinness had an immediate and inexplicable sense of foreboding upon seeing the car. He told Dean, "Please, never get in it. If you get in that car, you will be found dead in it by this time next week."

Dean, known for his rebellious persona both on and off screen, laughed off the warning. He reportedly responded with characteristic bravado, dismissing Guinness's concerns.

Tragically, Guinness's premonition proved to be chillingly accurate. On September 30, 1955, exactly seven days after the encounter, James Dean was involved in a fatal car accident while driving the Porsche 550 Spyder. The crash occurred near Cholame, California, when Dean's Porsche collided with a Ford Tudor sedan at an intersection. Dean was pronounced dead on arrival at the hospital.

The eerie accuracy of Guinness's prediction has led many to speculate about the nature of premonitions and the concept of "cursed" objects. The story has become a part of Hollywood lore, often recounted as an example of inexplicable foresight or a tragic twist of fate.

In the years following the accident, stories circulated about the "curse" of Dean's Porsche. Parts of the wrecked car were reportedly used in other vehicles, which were then involved in accidents. While many of these tales are likely exaggerations or urban legends, they have contributed to the mystique surrounding Dean's last ride.

The story of James Dean's Porsche serves as a haunting reminder of the fragility of life and the unpredictable nature of fate. It continues to fascinate people, blending elements of celebrity, tragedy, and the supernatural into a compelling narrative that has stood the test of time.

Chapter Twelve

The Hoover Dam Workers: A 13-Year Cycle of Tragedy

The construction of the Hoover Dam, one of the most ambitious engineering projects of the 20th century, is a tale of human perseverance and technological triumph. However, embedded within this narrative of progress is a haunting coincidence that spans 13 years and links the first and last fatalities of the dam's construction.

The Hoover Dam, originally known as Boulder Dam, was built between 1931 and 1936 during the Great Depression. The massive structure, designed to tame the Colorado River and provide water and electricity to the American Southwest, required the labor of thousands of workers under often dangerous conditions.

The first fatality associated with the dam's construction occurred on December 20, 1922, even before official work on the dam had begun. J.G. Tierney, a surveyor working for the U.S. Bureau of Reclamation, was scouting the Black Canyon for an ideal location for the dam. He was riding in a barge on the Colorado River when it capsized. Tierney drowned in the swift currents of the river, becoming the project's first casualty.

Fast forward 13 years to December 20, 1935. The dam was nearing completion, with only final touches remaining. On this day, Patrick Tierney, an electrician's helper, was working on an intake tower when he fell to his death. In a tragic twist of fate, Patrick was the son of J.G. Tierney, the surveyor who had died 13 years earlier to the day.

The coincidence is striking not just because of the family connection, but also due to the exact 13-year span between the two deaths, and the fact that they occurred on the same calendar date. This eerie symmetry has led many to view the Tierney deaths as more than mere coincidence, seeing in them a sort of cosmic bookending of the dam's human cost.

Over the course of its construction, the Hoover Dam claimed the lives of 96 workers, according to official records. Unofficial estimates place the number higher, possibly over 100. These deaths were due to various causes including falling rocks or debris, drowning, falls from the canyon walls, and even carbon monoxide poisoning.

The story of the Tierneys serves as a poignant reminder of the human sacrifice involved in creating one of America's most iconic structures. It highlights the dangers faced by the workers who built the dam and the personal tragedies that often get overshadowed by the grandeur of such massive projects.

Today, the Hoover Dam stands not only as a testament to human engineering and ambition but also as a memorial to those who lost their lives in its creation. The coincidence of the Tierney deaths, spanning the entire construction period, adds a layer of mythic resonance to the dam's already impressive history.

Chapter Thirteen

The Stoneman Coincidence: A Tale of Delayed Fate

The story of Henry Ziegland is a tale that seems to defy the laws of probability, blending elements of romance, tragedy, and an almost karmic sense of delayed justice. This extraordinary series of events, which unfolded in Honey Grove, Texas, spans decades and culminates in one of the most bizarre coincidences in recorded history.

The story begins in 1883 when Henry Ziegland callously broke off his relationship with his girlfriend. Devastated by the breakup, the young woman took her own life. Her brother, driven by grief and anger, sought revenge. He tracked down Ziegland and, believing he had killed him, turned the gun on himself and committed suicide.

However, unbeknownst to the brother, his attempt at vengeance had failed. The bullet had only grazed Ziegland's face before lodging in a nearby tree. Ziegland, having narrowly escaped death, likely thought the matter was closed. He went on with his life, perhaps considering himself lucky to have survived the encounter.

Fast forward to 1913, thirty years after the initial incident. Ziegland was clearing some land on his property and decided to remove a large tree - the very same tree that had stopped the bullet meant to kill him three decades earlier. The tree proved stubborn, resisting traditional methods of removal. Ziegland, in a decision that would prove fateful, decided to use dynamite to blast the tree apart.

When the dynamite detonated, it dislodged the bullet that had been embedded in the tree for thirty years. In an incredible twist of fate, the freed bullet struck Ziegland in the head, killing him instantly. The bullet that was meant to end his life in 1883 had finally found its mark in 1913.

This extraordinary chain of events raises questions about the nature of fate, coincidence, and justice. Was it mere chance that the bullet finally found its target after so many years? Or was there some greater force at work, ensuring that Ziegland ultimately paid for his callous behavior?

The Ziegland story has been retold many times over the years, often embellished or altered in the telling. While the exact details may be difficult to verify, the core of the story - a man killed by a bullet fired decades earlier - remains a compelling tale of delayed retribution.

This incident serves as a reminder of the unpredictable nature of life and death. It suggests that our actions, no matter how far in the past, can have unforeseen consequences. The Stoneman coincidence continues to captivate those who hear it, serving as a modern-day parable about fate, karma, and the long arc of justice.

Chapter Fourteen

The Identical Book Misprint: A Publisher's Nightmare

In the world of publishing, misprints and errors are not uncommon. However, the case of the identical book misprint that occurred in 1973 is a coincidence so extraordinary that it defies logical explanation. This incident involves two separate books, published by different companies, that contained the exact same typographical error on the exact same page.

The story begins with two books: "The Decade of Destruction" by Lewis Zickel and "The Day of St. Anthony's Fire" by John G. Fuller. These books were entirely different in subject matter and were published by two distinct publishing houses. "The Decade of Destruction" was a history book, while "The Day of St. Anthony's Fire" was about a mysterious illness that struck a French town in 1951.

Despite their differences, both books contained an identical error on page 40. In both cases, the word "skein" was misprinted as "skain." This might not seem particularly remarkable at first glance - after all, typos happen. But the coincidence deepens when we consider the context.

The word "skein" is not a common one. It refers to a length of thread or yarn, loosely coiled and knotted. For this unusual word to be misspelled in the exact same way, on the exact same page number, in two unrelated books published around the same time, is a coincidence of staggering improbability.

When this error was discovered, it caused quite a stir in the publishing world. Experts were baffled by the similarity of the mistakes. Some speculated that perhaps the same typesetter had worked on both books, but this theory was quickly disproven when it was confirmed that the books were produced by entirely separate publishing houses with no overlap in staff.

The incident raised questions about the nature of coincidence and the potential for seemingly impossible events to occur. It challenged our understanding of probability and randomness, suggesting that even in a field as controlled and scrutinized as book publishing, inexplicable parallels can emerge.

This case has since become a favorite anecdote among publishers, editors, and bibliophiles. It serves as a humbling reminder that no matter how careful we are, errors can slip through - and sometimes, these errors can align in ways that seem to defy explanation.

The identical book misprint remains one of the most puzzling coincidences in publishing history. It continues to intrigue those who hear about it, serving as a testament to the unpredictable and sometimes seemingly impossible nature of coincidence. Whether viewed as a quirk of probability or something more mysterious, this incident reminds us that truth can indeed be stranger than fiction.

Chapter Fifteen

The Dennis the Menace Coincidence: Transatlantic Twins

In the annals of comic strip history, few coincidences are as striking as the simultaneous creation of two mischievous characters named Dennis the Menace, on opposite sides of the Atlantic Ocean. This remarkable incident occurred on March 12, 1951, when two cartoonists, working independently and unaware of each other, gave birth to their identically named protagonists.

In the United States, Hank Ketcham created his version of Dennis the Menace. Ketcham's Dennis was a precocious, blond-haired boy with a knack for unintentionally causing trouble. The character was inspired by Ketcham's own son, Dennis, who had a reputation for mischief.

On the very same day, across the Atlantic in the United Kingdom, cartoonist David Law introduced his own Dennis the Menace in the children's comic magazine "The Beano." Law's Dennis was a dark-haired troublemaker with a malevolent streak, quite different in appearance and temperament from his American namesake.

The coincidence is made even more remarkable by the fact that the term "menace" was not commonly used to describe troublesome children at the time. For two cartoonists to independently come up with the same descriptive name for their characters on the same day is a coincidence of staggering improbability.

Neither Ketcham nor Law was aware of the other's creation until their respective strips had been running for several months. By then, both Dennis the Menaces had already gained popularity in their home countries.

The simultaneous creation led to an interesting copyright situation. While the characters shared a name, their distinct appearances and personalities meant that both could coexist without infringing on each other's rights. In fact, the two Dennises went on to become beloved characters in their respective countries, each developing a unique legacy.

This coincidence has fascinated comic enthusiasts and statisticians alike. It raises questions about the nature of creativity and the potential for simultaneous invention. Some have speculated about a collective unconscious or zeitgeist that might have influenced both artists, while others view it as a simple, albeit extraordinary, coincidence.

The Dennis the Menace incident serves as a reminder of the unpredictable nature of creative endeavors. It shows how similar ideas can emerge independently in different parts of the world, shaped by their unique cultural contexts.

Today, both Dennis the Menace comics continue to be published, delighting readers on both sides of the Atlantic. Their simultaneous creation remains one of the most remarkable coincidences in the history of comics, a testament to the sometimes inexplicable synchronicities that can occur in human creativity.

Chapter Sixteen

The King's Cross Fire Prophecy: A Psychic's Chilling Prediction

The King's Cross fire of 1987 remains one of the most tragic events in London's history. But what makes this incident even more chilling is the alleged prophecy that preceded it, adding a layer of eerie foresight to an already devastating occurrence.

On November 18, 1987, a fire broke out at King's Cross St Pancras tube station, one of London's busiest underground stations. The blaze, which started on an escalator, quickly spread, resulting in 31 deaths and injuring over 100 people. It was the deadliest fire in the history of the London Underground.

What sets this tragedy apart is the claim of a psychic prediction made just hours before the fire erupted. Suzanne Fountain, a psychic medium, reportedly had a vivid vision of a major fire at the station earlier that same day.

According to accounts, Fountain was traveling on the Piccadilly Line when she experienced an overwhelming sense of heat and smoke. She described seeing flames and people running in panic. Deeply disturbed by this vision, Fountain reportedly tried to warn station staff about the impending disaster.

Unfortunately, her warnings were not heeded. Like many claimed psychic predictions, they were likely dismissed as the ravings of an overactive imagination. Tragically, just hours later, Fountain's vision became a horrifying reality.

The timing and specificity of Fountain's alleged prediction have led many to view it as more than mere coincidence. Skeptics, however, point out that psychic predictions are often vague or reinterpreted after the fact to fit events. They argue that in a busy city like London, warnings of potential disasters are not uncommon.

Regardless of one's beliefs about psychic phenomena, the King's Cross fire prophecy raises intriguing questions about precognition and the nature of time. Could Fountain have somehow glimpsed the future? Or was this simply a tragic coincidence?

The incident has become a part of London's urban folklore, often discussed alongside other claimed premonitions of disasters. It serves as a haunting reminder of the unpredictability of tragedy and the human desire to find meaning and pattern in random events.

Today, the King's Cross fire is remembered not only for its tragic toll but also for the safety improvements it prompted in the London Underground. And for some, it remains a chilling example of the mysteries that continue to surround psychic predictions and their occasional, unsettling accuracy.

Last edited 49 minutes ago

Chapter Seventeen

The Fibonacci Birthdays: Nature's Sequence in Human Birth

In the realm of mathematical coincidences, few stories are as captivating as the case of the Fibonacci birthdays. This extraordinary event, which occurred in 2014, saw the birth weights of three siblings align perfectly with one of nature's most famous numerical sequences.

The Fibonacci sequence is a series of numbers where each number is the sum of the two preceding ones. It typically starts with 0 and 1, and continues as 1, 2, 3, 5, 8, 13, and so on. This sequence appears frequently in nature, from the spiral of shells to the arrangement of leaves on a stem.

In 2014, a woman in Clarksville, Tennessee, gave birth to three children on three consecutive days. What made this already unusual occurrence truly remarkable was the pattern of the babies' birth weights. The first child weighed 7 pounds, 11 ounces (7.7 lbs), the second 5 pounds, 7 ounces (5.7 lbs), and the third 3 pounds, 7 ounces (3.7 lbs).

When converted to a decimal format, these weights form the sequence 7.7, 5.7, 3.7. This mirrors a section of the Fibonacci sequence, where each number is the sum of the two that follow it. In this case, 7.7 = 5.7 + 3.7 (allowing for a small rounding error).

The odds of this happening by chance are astronomical. Not only did the mother give birth on three consecutive days (a rare event in itself), but the babies' weights also aligned with a mathematical sequence that has fascinated scholars for centuries.

This coincidence caught the attention of mathematicians and statisticians worldwide. It was seen as a striking example of how patterns that govern the natural world can sometimes manifest in unexpected ways in human affairs.

Some viewed this event as mere chance, a quirk of probability in a world full of births. Others saw it as evidence of the deep, underlying mathematical principles that govern our universe, appearing even in such seemingly random events as human birth weights.

The story of the Fibonacci birthdays serves as a reminder of the unexpected ways in which mathematics can intersect with our daily lives. It highlights the human tendency to seek and find patterns, even in the most unlikely places.

Whether viewed as a mathematical miracle or a fascinating fluke, the Fibonacci birthdays remain a captivating example of how the abstract world of numbers can sometimes align perfectly with the messy realities of human life.

Chapter Eighteen

The Identical Lottery Numbers: A Statistical Anomaly in Bulgaria

In the world of lottery drawings, where randomness and unpredictability are paramount, the events that unfolded in the Bulgarian lottery in 2009 stand out as a statistical anomaly so improbable that it sparked accusations of fraud and manipulation.

On September 6, 2009, the Bulgarian lottery drew the winning numbers for its 6/42 game. The numbers were 4, 15, 23, 24, 35, and 42. Just four days later, on September 10, the lottery drew its numbers again. In an astounding turn of events, the exact same sequence of numbers was drawn: 4, 15, 23, 24, 35, and 42.

The odds of this happening by chance are astronomical. Mathematicians calculated the probability at 1 in 4.2 million, and that's just for two consecutive draws. The fact that it happened within the same week made it even more incredible.

As news of this extraordinary coincidence spread, reactions ranged from disbelief to suspicion. Many lottery players were stunned, while others cried foul. The Bulgarian authorities found themselves under intense scrutiny, facing accusations of fraud or a flawed lottery system.

In response to the public outcry, the Bulgarian Sports Minister at the time, Svilen Neykov, ordered an investigation into the draw. He stated,

"This is happening for the first time in the 52-year history of the lottery. We are absolutely stunned to see such a freak coincidence, but we are dealing with a game of chance, after all."

Lottery officials maintained that the draw was conducted fairly and that the repeated numbers were simply an extraordinary coincidence. They pointed out that, theoretically, such an event could happen, even if the odds were extremely low.

The investigation ultimately found no evidence of wrongdoing. The lottery machine and the balls used in the draw were examined and found to be functioning correctly. Despite this, many remained skeptical, finding it hard to accept that such an improbable event could occur by chance.

This incident sparked discussions about the nature of randomness and probability. Statisticians pointed out that while such an event is highly unlikely, given the number of lottery draws that happen worldwide, it's not impossible for such coincidences to occur occasionally.

The Bulgarian lottery incident serves as a stark reminder of the counter-intuitive nature of probability. It highlights how events that seem almost impossible can and do happen, challenging our intuitions about chance and randomness.

Today, the case of the repeated Bulgarian lottery numbers remains a fascinating example of an extreme statistical anomaly. It continues to be discussed in probability classes and cited in discussions about the nature of randomness and the occurrence of highly improbable events.

Chapter Nineteen

The Falling Cats Coincidence: A Feline Tale Spanning Generations

In the realm of historical coincidences, few stories are as peculiar and thought-provoking as the tale of the falling cats in Bordentown, New Jersey. This bizarre incident spans nearly a century and involves two generations of the same family, challenging our understanding of probability and the nature of coincidence.

The story begins in 1894. A man was walking past a tall building in Bordentown when, in a freak accident, a cat fell from an upper window. In a tragic twist of fate, the falling feline struck the pedestrian, killing him instantly. This unusual death made local headlines and was remembered as one of the strangest accidents in the town's history.

Fast forward to 1977, approximately 83 years later. The grandson of the original victim was walking down the very same street in Bordentown. In an almost unbelievable repetition of history, another cat fell from a building, striking and killing the grandson. The eerie similarity to his grandfather's death decades earlier stunned the local community and soon captured national attention.

The odds of such an event occurring once are slim; for it to happen twice to members of the same family, in the same location, generations apart, seems to defy probability. This coincidence raises questions about the nature of fate, family curses, and the mysterious patterns that sometimes seem to emerge in the chaos of life.

Skeptics might argue that given enough time and enough events, even the most improbable coincidences will eventually occur. They might point out that cats falling from buildings in urban areas, while uncommon, is not unheard of. However, the specific details of this case - the family connection, the same location, and the fatal outcome - make it particularly striking.

The story of the falling cats has since become a part of Bordentown's local lore, often recounted as an example of truth being stranger than fiction. It has been featured in books about historical coincidences and is often cited in discussions about the nature of probability and chance.

This incident serves as a reminder of the unpredictable and sometimes seemingly impossible nature of life. It challenges our understanding of randomness and makes us question whether there might be unseen patterns or forces at work in the universe.

Whether viewed as a tragic coincidence or something more mysterious, the tale of the falling cats of Bordentown continues to fascinate and perplex those who hear it. It stands as a testament to the fact that history, on rare occasions, can repeat itself in the most unexpected and extraordinary ways.

Chapter Twenty

The Reincarnation Coincidence: A Tale of Two Brothers

In the realm of reincarnation stories, few are as compelling and specific as the case that unfolded in Coatbridge, Scotland, in the mid-20th century. This extraordinary tale involves two brothers, separated by death, yet seemingly connected across time in a way that challenges our understanding of life and death.

The story begins in 1957 when a young boy named John was tragically hit and killed by a van in the town of Coatbridge. The loss devastated his family, particularly his younger brother, who was born two years after John's death.

As this younger brother grew, he began to exhibit behaviors and knowledge that seemed impossible for him to have acquired naturally. He would often talk about John's life with an uncanny level of detail and accuracy. He spoke of events and experiences that had occurred before he was born as if he had lived them himself.

The situation took an even more extraordinary turn when, in 1971, the younger brother, now a teenager, was involved in a fatal accident. In a chilling echo of his older brother's death, he too was struck and killed by a vehicle.

The coincidence deepened when it was discovered that the driver involved in this second accident shared the same name as the driver who had killed John 14 years earlier. While it wasn't the same individual, the identical name added another layer of eerie similarity to the two tragedies.

This case has been widely discussed in parapsychological circles and among those interested in reincarnation. Some view it as compelling evidence for the existence of past lives, suggesting that John's consciousness somehow transferred to his younger brother. They point to the detailed knowledge the younger brother had of John's life as proof of this transfer.

Skeptics, however, offer alternative explanations. They suggest that the younger brother might have absorbed information about John through family stories and photographs, unconsciously constructing a narrative that he came to believe was his own past life. The coincidence of the drivers' names, they argue, is just that – a coincidence, albeit a remarkably unlikely one.

Regardless of one's beliefs about reincarnation, this case presents a fascinating study in family dynamics, grief, and the human tendency to seek meaning in tragedy. It raises profound questions about the nature of consciousness, memory, and the bonds that connect us to our loved ones.

The Coatbridge reincarnation case remains one of the most intriguing and well-documented instances of supposed past-life recall. It continues to challenge our understanding of life, death, and the possibility of consciousness persisting beyond the grave.

Chapter Twenty-One

The Lightning Strike Survivor: Roy Sullivan's Shocking Tale

In the annals of improbable events, the story of Roy Sullivan stands out as truly electrifying. Known as the "Human Lightning Rod," Sullivan, a park ranger in Shenandoah National Park, Virginia, survived being struck by lightning an astonishing seven times between 1942 and 1977.

Roy Cleveland Sullivan was born in Greene County, Virginia, in 1912. He began working as a park ranger in 1936, a job that kept him outdoors and, unknowingly, put him at increased risk of lightning strikes. His first recorded strike occurred in 1942 when a lightning bolt hit a fire lookout tower he was in, setting it on fire. Sullivan ran out of the tower, but was struck again just outside it, burning off a strip of hair on his leg.

This was just the beginning of Sullivan's shocking experiences. His second strike came in 1969 while he was driving his truck on a mountain road. The bolt knocked him unconscious and burned off his eyebrows and eyelashes. In 1970, a third strike hit him in his front yard, injuring his left shoulder.

The fourth strike in 1972 set his hair on fire while he was working inside a ranger station. In 1973, while he was on patrol in the park, Sullivan saw a storm cloud forming and tried to outrun it in his truck. The fifth strike hit him through the open window of his truck, once again setting his hair on fire.

The sixth strike came in 1976 while he was checking on a campground. It injured his ankle. The seventh and final recorded strike occurred in 1977 while Sullivan was fishing in a freshwater pool. This time, he suffered chest and stomach burns.

Unsurprisingly, Sullivan's experiences made him somewhat wary of storms. He reportedly began to believe that some force was trying to destroy him. In a sad twist of fate, Roy Sullivan died in 1983 from a self-inflicted gunshot wound, reportedly due to unrequited love.

Sullivan's incredible story has been recognized by Guinness World Records for the most lightning strikes survived by one person. It has also been the subject of numerous articles, books, and discussions in the scientific community.

While some skeptics have questioned the veracity of all seven strikes, the evidence – including burn marks and witnesses – supports Sullivan's claims. His story serves as a reminder of the unpredictable nature of lightning and the importance of safety during storms.

The tale of Roy Sullivan, the Human Lightning Rod, continues to fascinate people around the world. It stands as a testament to human resilience and the sometimes unbelievable twists that fate can take.

Chapter Twenty-Two

The Linked Lottery Winners: A Tale of Brotherly Fortune

In the world of lottery wins, coincidences are bound to happen. But few are as remarkable as the story of two brothers from the United Kingdom who both won the lottery on the same day in 2005, defying astronomical odds and capturing the public's imagination.

The protagonists of this extraordinary tale are James and Bob Stocklas, two brothers from Pennsylvania who had always been close. On March 4, 2005, their bond was strengthened in a way neither could have imagined.

James, a judge from Bethlehem, Pennsylvania, was on his annual fishing trip in Florida when he decided to buy a lottery ticket. Meanwhile, back in Pennsylvania, his brother Bob also chose to try his luck with the lottery.

When the numbers were drawn, both brothers were shocked to discover they had won. But the real surprise came when they realized they had won on the same day, in different states, with different lottery games.

James hit the jackpot, winning a staggering $291 million in the Florida Powerball lottery. Bob's win was considerably more modest – just $7 in a Pennsylvania lottery scratch-off game. Despite the vast difference in their winnings, both brothers were elated at their simultaneous good fortune.

The odds of two brothers winning any prize in the lottery on the same day are incredibly small. When you factor in James's massive jackpot win, the coincidence becomes even more remarkable.

This story captured media attention worldwide, with many people fascinated by the brothers' linked luck. It sparked discussions about the nature of probability and the role of chance in our lives. Some saw it as evidence of a special connection between the brothers, while others viewed it simply as an extraordinary coincidence.

James, for his part, didn't forget his brother in the excitement of his win. In a gesture that speaks volumes about their relationship, he flew Bob to Florida on a private jet to collect his winnings together. The image of the two brothers holding their vastly different checks became iconic, symbolizing both the randomness of luck and the enduring nature of family bonds.

Chapter Twenty-Three

The Titanic Survivor's Luck: Violet Jessop's Incredible Tale

In the annals of maritime history, few stories are as remarkable as that of Violet Jessop, a ship stewardess who survived not one, but three major ship disasters in the early 20th century, including the infamous sinking of the Titanic.

Violet Constance Jessop was born in 1887 in Argentina to Irish immigrants. She began her career as an ocean liner stewardess in 1908, working for the White Star Line. Little did she know that her career would lead her into the path of some of the most dramatic maritime disasters of her time.

Her first brush with disaster came in 1911 when she was working aboard the RMS Olympic, sister ship to the Titanic. The Olympic collided with the HMS Hawke near the Isle of Wight. While the ship was badly damaged, it managed to limp back to port, and no lives were lost. Jessop, unperturbed by this incident, continued her career at sea.

The next year, in 1912, Jessop was assigned to the maiden voyage of the RMS Titanic. On April 14, the Titanic struck an iceberg and began to sink. Jessop was ordered into lifeboat 16 and, as the ship went down, she watched the unfolding tragedy. She was one of the fortunate survivors rescued by the Carpathia.

Most people would have given up seafaring after such a traumatic experience, but not Violet Jessop. She returned to work, this time as a nurse for the British Red Cross during World War I. It was in this capacity that she found herself aboard the HMHS Britannic, the third of the Olympic-class liners.

On November 21, 1916, the Britannic struck a mine laid by a German U-boat and sank in the Aegean Sea. Once again, Jessop found herself evacuating a sinking ship. She nearly lost her life when her lifeboat was sucked into the Britannic's still-turning propellers, but she managed to jump clear just in time. She was rescued from the water, suffering a serious head injury, but alive.

Incredibly, Jessop's experiences did not deter her from her maritime career. She continued to work on ships well into the 1950s. She wrote her memoirs, titled "Titanic Survivor," which were published posthumously in 1997.

Violet Jessop's story is one of remarkable resilience and perhaps a touch of incredible luck. Her survival of three major maritime disasters, including the most famous shipwreck in history, has made her a legend in seafaring lore. Her tale serves as a testament to human endurance and the unpredictable nature of fate.

Today, Jessop is remembered not only for her extraordinary experiences but also for her courage and dedication to her profession despite the dangers she faced. Her story continues to fascinate maritime historians and the public alike, a remarkable tale of survival against seemingly impossible odds.

Chapter Twenty-Four

The Balloon Release Coincidence: A Transatlantic Connection

In 1998, a heartwarming coincidence occurred that seemed to defy the odds, connecting two young girls across the vast expanse of the Atlantic Ocean. This remarkable story begins in the town of Pewsey, Wiltshire, in southwest England.

Laura Buxton, a 10-year-old girl, was attending a neighbor's 50th wedding anniversary celebration. As part of the festivities, Laura released a helium balloon into the sky. Attached to the balloon was a small label with her name and address, along with a request for the finder to write back.

The balloon traveled northeast, crossing over the English Channel and the North Sea. It drifted for nearly 140 miles before descending in a field in Lichtfield, a village in Staffordshire, England. Here's where the story takes an incredible turn.

The balloon was found by a man who lived next door to another young girl named Laura Buxton. Yes, you read that correctly – the finder's neighbor shared the exact same name as the girl who had released the balloon. This second Laura Buxton was also 10 years old.

Thinking the balloon was intended for his young neighbor, the man passed it along to her. When the second Laura Buxton received the balloon and saw the name on the label, she was understandably confused. She wrote back to the address, beginning a correspondence that would reveal the extraordinary nature of this coincidence.

As the two girls began to exchange letters, they discovered more similarities beyond their shared name and age. Both were fair-haired and about the same height. Both owned guinea pigs as pets. Both had three-year-old black Labradors. And when they finally met in person, they even showed up wearing similar outfits – a pink sweater and jeans.

The odds of this series of coincidences are truly astronomical. For a balloon to travel such a distance and be found at all is unlikely enough. For it to be found near someone with the exact same name and age as the sender, and for the two girls to share so many other similarities, seems to stretch the bounds of probability.

This story captured media attention and public imagination, sparking discussions about the nature of coincidence and the interconnectedness of our world. Some saw it as mere chance, while others interpreted it as evidence of some greater pattern or design in the universe.

The balloon release coincidence serves as a heartwarming reminder of the unexpected connections that can form between people. It stands as a testament to the sometimes inexplicable nature of coincidence and the joy that can come from embracing these unlikely occurrences.

Today, the story of the two Laura Buxtons continues to be recounted as one of the most remarkable coincidences in recent memory, a tale that seems to bridge the gap between everyday life and the realm of the extraordinary.

Chapter Twenty-Five

The Identical Hotel Rooms: A Case of Double Booking

In the world of hotel management, double bookings are an occasional, if inconvenient, occurrence. But the case of the identical hotel rooms that unfolded in a Midwest American hotel in the early 2000s takes the concept of a booking mix-up to an entirely new level.

The incident occurred when two men, both named John Smith (a common name, but crucial to this story), checked into the same hotel on the same day. This alone isn't particularly unusual - John Smith is, after all, one of the most common names in the English-speaking world. However, what happened next defies ordinary probability.

Due to a glitch in the hotel's computer system, both John Smiths were accidentally assigned to the same room. This type of error is typically caught quickly, either by the front desk staff or by the guests themselves. But in this case, an extraordinary series of events allowed the mistake to go unnoticed for several hours.

The first John Smith arrived at the hotel in the early afternoon and checked in without incident. He went to his assigned room, unpacked, and then left to attend a business meeting. The second John Smith arrived in the early evening. He too was given a key to the same room and proceeded upstairs.

When the second Mr. Smith entered the room, he was initially confused by the presence of someone else's belongings. However, in a remarkable twist, he soon convinced himself that the items must be his own. The suitcase was similar to his, and the clothes inside were of the same general style and size he wore.

The true nature of the mix-up only came to light when the first John Smith returned to the room late that night, leading to a confusing and somewhat comical confrontation between the two men. Hotel staff were quickly called to sort out the situation.

As the story unfolded, more coincidences came to light. Not only did the two men share the same name, but they were also both visiting from New York City, both worked as salesmen, and both were born on the same day (although in different years). These shared characteristics had contributed to the computer glitch that assigned them the same room.

This incident serves as a remarkable example of how a series of small coincidences can compound to create a truly extraordinary situation. It highlights the potential for technology to amplify human error in unexpected ways, and the strange scenarios that can unfold when chance aligns just right.

The tale of the identical hotel rooms has since become a favorite anecdote in hospitality management training, a reminder of the importance of double-checking bookings and the unpredictable nature of the hotel business. It stands as a testament to the sometimes bizarre coincidences that can occur in our daily lives, turning an ordinary hotel stay into an unforgettable story of mistaken identity and serendipity.

Chapter Twenty-Six

The Hemingway Lightning: A Writer's Prophetic Boast

Ernest Hemingway, the legendary American author known for his terse prose and adventurous lifestyle, was no stranger to danger. But one of his boasts, made in jest, would later take on an eerie, almost prophetic quality that continues to intrigue literary enthusiasts and coincidence seekers alike.

Hemingway had a well-known fascination with death, often incorporating themes of mortality into his writing. This preoccupation extended to his personal life, where he was known to make bold, sometimes morbid statements. One such claim was that he could "walk safely between the raindrops" of a lightning storm.

This boast wasn't just idle talk. Hemingway had survived numerous close calls throughout his life, including plane crashes, car accidents, and wartime injuries. His ability to emerge unscathed from dangerous situations had become almost legendary among his friends and admirers.

However, fate had a cruel irony in store for the great writer. On July 2, 1961, Hemingway took his own life with a shotgun at his home in Ketchum, Idaho. What makes this tragic event particularly chilling is that at the time of his death, a violent thunderstorm was raging outside.

The juxtaposition of Hemingway's suicide and the thunderstorm outside created a haunting parallel to his earlier boast. It was as if, in his final moments, the writer who had so often courted danger and defied death had finally succumbed, not to the lightning he claimed he could avoid, but to his own hand.

This coincidence has been the subject of much discussion among Hemingway scholars and biographers. Some see it as a final, tragic irony in the life of a man who had built his reputation on facing danger head-on. Others view it as a poignant metaphor for Hemingway's lifelong struggle with depression and his ultimate inability to outrun his inner demons.

The image of Hemingway ending his life while a storm raged outside has become an enduring part of the author's mythology. It speaks to the complex relationship between the writer's life and his art, where the boundaries between reality and fiction often blurred.

This coincidence serves as a somber reminder of the unpredictability of life and death, and how even those who seem invincible can be vulnerable. It adds a layer of tragic poetry to the end of one of America's greatest writers, a man who lived life on his own terms and, in the end, chose to leave it the same way.

The story of Hemingway's lightning continues to fascinate, a stark example of how life can sometimes mirror art in the most unexpected and poignant ways.

Chapter Twenty-Seven

The Separated Book: A Literary Reunion Across Time

In the realm of coincidences, few stories are as heartwarming and unlikely as the tale of a man who unknowingly bought a book that once belonged to his wife, long before they had ever met. This extraordinary event, which occurred in the early 2000s, serves as a testament to the strange ways in which objects can connect people across time and space.

The story begins with a man browsing a used bookstore, a common pastime for book lovers. As he perused the shelves, a particular book caught his eye. It was nothing extraordinary - just a used paperback novel - but something about it appealed to him. He purchased the book and took it home, looking forward to reading it.

When he opened the book, however, he found something unexpected. On the inside cover was a handwritten name - a name he recognized instantly. It was his wife's name, written in her distinctive handwriting.

Intrigued and a little confused, he showed the book to his wife. She was equally surprised and confirmed that it was indeed her handwriting. As they discussed the strange coincidence, they realized that this book was one she had owned as a child, long before they had ever met.

The book had somehow made its way from his wife's childhood home, through various hands and possibly multiple bookstores, only to end up being purchased by her future husband decades later. The odds of this happening are incredibly small, especially considering that the couple had grown up in different parts of the country.

This serendipitous event sparked a wave of nostalgia for the wife, bringing back memories of her childhood reading experiences. For the husband, it created a unique connection to his wife's past, allowing him to hold a piece of her history that predated their relationship.

The story quickly spread among their friends and family, with many viewing it as a sign that the couple was truly meant to be together. Some saw it as evidence of fate or destiny, while others simply marveled at the incredible chain of events that led to this moment.

This tale of the separated book serves as a poignant reminder of the interconnectedness of our lives and the objects that pass through them. It highlights how seemingly random choices - like picking up a particular book in a store - can lead to profound discoveries and connections.

Moreover, this coincidence speaks to the enduring power of books to connect people, not just through the stories they tell, but through their physical journey through the world. In an age of digital media, this story underscores the unique value of physical books as carriers of both stories and personal histories.

The separated book reunion remains a favorite anecdote for those who love stories of serendipity and coincidence. It stands as a heartwarming example of how the past and present can intersect in the most unexpected ways, creating moments of wonder and connection in our daily lives.

Chapter Twenty-Eight

The Futurama Prediction: When Animation Imitates Life

In the realm of pop culture coincidences, few are as eerily precise as the case of the animated series "Futurama" predicting a real-life event years before it occurred. This instance of art seemingly foreseeing reality has fascinated fans and skeptics alike, blurring the lines between fiction and fact in an uncanny way.

"Futurama," created by Matt Groening (also known for "The Simpsons"), is a science fiction animated comedy set in the 31st century. The show is known for its clever writing, which often includes scientific and mathematical jokes and references. But one particular episode, which aired in 1999, contained a detail that would prove to be remarkably prescient.

In the episode titled "Space Pilot 3000," the main character, Fry, is a pizza delivery boy who accidentally gets cryogenically frozen on New Year's Eve 1999. When he wakes up in the year 3000, he finds himself in a futuristic world full of advanced technology and alien life forms.

The coincidence lies in a small detail of Fry's last delivery before being frozen. He is sent to deliver a pizza to a cryogenics lab, to a customer named "I.C. Wiener" (obviously a prank name). When Fry arrives at the lab, he finds it empty and ends up falling into a cryogenic pod himself.

Fast forward to 2014, when a man named John Weiner (pronounced the same as "wiener") opened a cryogenics lab called Peacefulpod Cryonics in Culver City, California. The similarity between the fictional "I.C. Wiener" ordering from a cryogenics lab and a real person named Weiner opening such a facility is striking.

When this coincidence was discovered, it quickly spread among "Futurama" fans and coincidence enthusiasts. Many were amazed at the specificity of the prediction - not just the concept of a cryogenics lab, which was already a part of scientific discourse in 1999, but the connection to a person named Weiner.

Skeptics, of course, point out that this is likely just a chance occurrence. The name "Wiener" is not uncommon, and cryonics has been a subject of scientific interest and speculation for decades. They argue that given the vast amount of content produced in television and other media, some coincidences with real-life events are bound to occur.

Nevertheless, this coincidence has become a favorite among "Futurama" fans and is often cited as an example of the show's "predictive" powers. It's worth noting that "The Simpsons," another Matt Groening creation, has also been credited with several apparent predictions of future events.

The Futurama prediction serves as a fascinating example of how fiction can sometimes align with future reality in unexpected ways. It highlights our human tendency to find patterns and meaning in coincidences, and the particular delight we take in instances of pop culture seemingly foreseeing real-world developments.

Chapter Twenty-Nine

The Coincidental Neighbors: A Birthday Surprise

In the tapestry of human connections, some threads intertwine in ways that seem too perfect to be mere chance. Such is the case of two women living in New Jersey, whose lives paralleled each other in an extraordinary series of coincidences that came to light in the early 2000s.

The story begins with two women who happened to be next-door neighbors in a suburban New Jersey town. Let's call them Sarah and Emily (names changed for privacy). Sarah and Emily were casual acquaintances, exchanging pleasantries over the fence and occasionally chatting at neighborhood gatherings. However, they were about to discover that their connection ran much deeper than they ever imagined.

The revelation came about during a conversation where birthdays came up. To their mutual surprise, Sarah and Emily discovered that they shared the same birthday - not just the same day and month, but the same year as well. Both women had been born on April 15, 1970.

Intrigued by this coincidence, they began to discuss the circumstances of their births. As they shared details, they were shocked to find out that they had been born not only on the same day but in the same hospital. Both women had entered the world at St. Mary's Hospital in Passaic, New Jersey.

The coincidences didn't stop there. As they delved deeper into their birth stories, they discovered that they had been delivered by the same doctor. Dr. Johnson (name changed) had presided over both of their births, bringing both Sarah and Emily into the world within hours of each other.

The odds of two people being born on the same day in the same year are already quite low. For them to be born in the same hospital, delivered by the same doctor, and then end up living next door to each other decades later stretches the boundaries of probability to an astounding degree.

This remarkable series of coincidences led Sarah and Emily to form a closer friendship, bonded by their shared history. They began celebrating their birthdays together and often joked about being "almost twins."

Their story quickly spread through their community and eventually caught the attention of local media. It served as a point of fascination for many, sparking discussions about fate, synchronicity, and the hidden connections that might exist between people.

Some saw it as mere chance - a fluke of statistics in a world of billions of people. Others viewed it as evidence of some greater design or purpose, a sign that Sarah and Emily were meant to be in each other's lives.

Regardless of how one interprets it, the story of these coincidental neighbors serves as a heartwarming reminder of the unexpected ways our lives can intersect with others. It highlights the potential for discovering profound connections in the most ordinary of circumstances and the joy that can come from recognizing these extraordinary coincidences in our lives.

Chapter Thirty

The Jeanne Calment Coincidence: A Lesson in Longevity

In the annals of human longevity, few names stand out as prominently as that of Jeanne Louise Calment. Born on February 21, 1875, in Arles, France, Calment lived to the astonishing age of 122 years and 164 days, making her the oldest verified person in recorded history. But it's not just her extreme longevity that makes her story remarkable - it's an incredible coincidence involving a real estate deal that spanned decades.

In 1965, at the age of 90, Jeanne Calment entered into an unusual real estate arrangement. She signed a deal with lawyer André-François Raffray, then aged 47, to sell her apartment to him on a contingency contract known in France as a "viager" deal. Under this agreement, Raffray would pay Calment a monthly sum of 2,500 francs (about $500 at the time) until her death, at which point he would inherit the apartment.

This type of arrangement was not uncommon in France, particularly for elderly individuals looking for a steady income in their later years. Typically, the buyer would expect to gain possession of the property within a few years, making it a potentially good investment.

However, Raffray couldn't have anticipated the extraordinary longevity of Madame Calment. Year after year, decade after decade, Calment continued to live, and Raffray continued to pay. By December 1995,

Raffray had paid Calment more than 930,000 francs, about double the apartment's value.

The incredible twist in this tale came when Raffray died in 1995 at the age of 77, having paid for the apartment for 30 years without ever taking possession of it. Even more remarkably, Calment outlived him by two years, passing away in 1997 at the age of 122.

This extraordinary coincidence turned what Raffray had likely seen as a sound investment into a financial loss for his estate. His widow was obligated to continue the payments until Calment's death, as per the original agreement.

Calment's longevity and the unfortunate timing for Raffray became a subject of fascination and amusement in France and beyond. It served as a poignant reminder of the unpredictability of life and death, and the risks inherent in making assumptions about longevity.

The story of Jeanne Calment and André-François Raffray has since become a cautionary tale in the world of French real estate, often cited as an extreme example of how "viager" deals can go wrong for the buyer. It's also seen as a humorous anecdote about the pitfalls of underestimating the elderly.

This remarkable coincidence not only highlights Calment's exceptional longevity but also serves as a fascinating case study in probability, risk, and the sometimes cruel ironies of fate. It remains one of the most extraordinary examples of how life can confound our expectations in the most unexpected ways.

Chapter Thirty-One

The Identical Tombstones: A Grave Coincidence

In the quiet confines of a cemetery in Vermont, a peculiar coincidence rests eternally, capturing the imagination of visitors and challenging our understanding of probability. This is the story of the identical tombstones - a tale of two men, unrelated in life, yet bound together in death by an extraordinary set of circumstances.

The story centers around two men, both named John Smith. While John Smith is a common name, what makes this case remarkable is the eerie similarity in the details of their lives and deaths, as recorded on their tombstones.

These two John Smiths lived and died in the same town in Vermont. What's truly astonishing is that they died on the exact same date. Their tombstones, placed side by side in the local cemetery, bear identical inscriptions:

"In memory of John Smith, who died on July 15, 1902, aged 57 years, 2 months, and 6 days."

The only difference between the two tombstones is the slight variation in the stonemason's carving style, suggesting they were crafted by different hands.

When this coincidence was discovered, it naturally led to much speculation and investigation. Local historians and curious visitors alike tried to uncover more about these two John Smiths. Despite extensive research, no familial connection between the two men could be found. They appeared to be, as far as anyone could determine, completely unrelated individuals who just happened to share a name, a death date, and even the exact same age at death.

The odds of two unrelated men with the same name dying on the same day at the same age are astronomically low. Add to this the fact that they were buried next to each other with identical tombstone inscriptions, and the coincidence becomes truly mind-boggling.

This unusual grave site has become something of a local legend, attracting curiosity seekers and coincidence enthusiasts from far and wide. It has sparked numerous theories and discussions about the nature of coincidence, fate, and the hidden patterns that might exist in our world.

Some view it as a simple, albeit remarkable, coincidence - a fluke of statistics in a world where millions of lives and deaths occur. Others see it as evidence of something more mysterious, perhaps a glitch in the matrix of reality or a sign of some greater cosmic order.

Regardless of how one interprets it, the story of the identical tombstones serves as a poignant reminder of the strange ways in which human lives can intersect, even beyond death. It challenges our notions of individuality and uniqueness, suggesting that even in the most personal details of our existence - our names, our lifespans, our final resting places - unexpected parallels can emerge.

This grave coincidence continues to fascinate those who encounter it, standing as a testament to the unpredictable and sometimes inexplicable nature of life and death. It remains one of the most curious and thought-provoking coincidences in cemetery lore, inviting us to ponder the mysterious threads that weave through the tapestry of human existence.

Chapter Thirty-Two

The Doppelgänger Plane Crash: A Chilling Repetition

In the annals of aviation history, there are many tragic stories. But few are as eerily coincidental as the tale of two plane crashes that occurred a decade apart, in the same location, with the same number of fatalities. This chilling repetition of history has become known as the Doppelgänger Plane Crash.

The first incident occurred on December 29, 1970. A Lockheed L-188A Electra aircraft, operated by LANSA (Líneas Aéreas Nacionales S. A.), was en route from Lima to Pucallpa, Peru. As the plane approached its destination, it encountered severe thunderstorms. The aircraft crashed into the dense Amazonian rainforest, killing 92 of the 93 people on board. The sole survivor was a 17-year-old girl named Juliane Koepcke, who fell 3 km (10,000 ft) still strapped to her seat and miraculously survived.

Fast forward to October 2, 1980. Another aircraft, this time a Lockheed L-188A Electra operated by Faucett Perú, was on the same route from Lima to Pucallpa. In a chilling echo of the previous crash, this plane also encountered bad weather near its destination. It too crashed into the rainforest, in almost the exact same location as the 1970 crash. Tragically, all 69 passengers and 6 crew members on board perished.

The similarities between these two crashes are striking:

1. Both involved the same type of aircraft (Lockheed L-188A Electra).

2. Both were on the same route (Lima to Pucallpa).

3. Both crashed in nearly the same location in the Amazonian rainforest.

4. Both occurred during bad weather conditions.

5. Both resulted in the deaths of all but one person in the first crash, and everyone in the second crash.

The odds of two such similar accidents occurring in the same place, under similar circumstances, are extraordinarily low. This coincidence has fascinated and puzzled aviation experts and coincidence enthusiasts alike.

Some have speculated about possible geographical or meteorological factors that might make this particular area especially dangerous for air travel. Others have pondered whether there might have been some common factor in the way the two flights were operated that contributed to both crashes.

However, official investigations into both incidents found different causes. The 1970 crash was attributed to a combination of bad weather and pilot error, while the 1980 crash was believed to be caused by an electrical failure that occurred during the storm.

This bizarre repetition of tragedy serves as a sobering reminder of the unpredictable nature of air travel and the sometimes inexplicable patterns that can emerge in disaster. It highlights how, despite advances in technology and safety measures, similar accidents can occur even years apart.

The Doppelgänger Plane Crash remains one of the most chilling coincidences in aviation history. It continues to be discussed and analyzed, a grim reminder of how history can sometimes repeat itself in the most tragic of ways.

Chapter Thirty-Three

The Defying Gravity Book: When Literature Takes a Literal Fall

In the world of literature, books are often described as having the power to move people. But in 2007, in a London bookstore, a book quite literally moved - and in doing so, created one of the most ironic and amusing coincidences in literary history.

The incident occurred in Waterstone's bookshop on Piccadilly in central London. On a seemingly ordinary day, a customer was browsing the science section of the store. Suddenly, without warning, a book fell from a high shelf, striking the unsuspecting browser on the head.

In any other circumstance, this might have been a simple accident, perhaps resulting in a minor bump and an apology from the staff. However, this was no ordinary book. The tome that decided to defy its shelf was a copy of "Gravity: How the Weakest Force in the Universe Shaped Our Lives" by Brian Clegg.

Yes, you read that correctly. A book about gravity chose that moment to demonstrate the very force it described by falling onto a customer's head.

The irony of the situation was not lost on anyone present. The customer, while slightly startled, was fortunately not hurt. In fact, reports suggest that once the initial shock wore off, both the customer and the bookstore staff found the incident highly amusing.

News of this coincidence quickly spread, first among the bookstore staff, then to other customers, and eventually to the media. It became a favorite anecdote in literary circles and among science enthusiasts, who appreciated the physical demonstration of the book's subject matter.

This incident serves as a humorous reminder of the unpredictable nature of coincidence. It also highlights how the universe sometimes seems to have a sense of humor, arranging events in ways that seem almost too perfect to be random.

From a scientific perspective, of course, there's nothing particularly special about a book on gravity falling. All books are subject to gravity equally. However, the human mind is wired to find meaning and patterns in events, which is why this particular incident stands out as remarkably coincidental.

The "Gravity" book incident has since become a beloved anecdote in the world of bookselling and publishing. It's often recounted as an example of life imitating art (or in this case, science), and as a reminder that sometimes, the most effective demonstrations of scientific principles come when we least expect them.

This coincidence also serves as a lighthearted reminder of the importance of proper shelving in bookstores. It's a tale that continues to bring smiles to faces of bibliophiles and scientists alike, a perfect blend of humor, irony, and the laws of physics in action.

Chapter Thirty-Four

The Life-Saving Swap: A Fateful Flight Change

In the realm of coincidences, few stories are as chilling and thought-provoking as the tale of two men who swapped flights at the last minute, unknowingly altering the course of their lives forever. This extraordinary event, which occurred in 1994, serves as a stark reminder of how small decisions can have life-changing consequences.

The story begins at Chicago's O'Hare International Airport. Two businessmen were waiting to board a flight to Atlanta, Georgia. Let's call them John and Mike (names changed for privacy). John and Mike didn't know each other, but they struck up a conversation while waiting at the gate.

As they chatted, they realized they were both heading to Atlanta for similar business meetings. However, Mike mentioned that he was hoping to get on an earlier flight to have more time to prepare for his meeting. John, who was in less of a rush, offered to swap tickets with Mike.

The airline staff were accommodating, and the swap was made. Mike boarded the earlier flight, while John waited for the later one. It seemed like a simple act of kindness between two strangers.

What happened next would haunt both men for years to come. The flight that Mike boarded - the one originally meant for John - crashed shortly after takeoff. There were no survivors.

John, who should have been on that ill-fated flight, watched the news in shock from the airport lounge. He realized that a chance encounter and a simple swap of tickets had saved his life. Meanwhile, Mike, who had been so eager to arrive in Atlanta early, had unknowingly boarded a doomed flight.

The incident raised profound questions about fate, chance, and the fragility of life. For John, it was a sobering reminder of how quickly everything can change. He was left to grapple with feelings of guilt and gratitude - grateful to be alive, but haunted by the thought that his survival came at the cost of another man's life.

This story quickly captured public attention, becoming a topic of discussion in media outlets and among those interested in tales of fate and coincidence. It led many to reflect on their own lives and the seemingly insignificant decisions that could have far-reaching consequences.

The life-saving swap serves as a powerful reminder of the unpredictability of life and death. It highlights how our paths can intersect with others in ways we can never anticipate, and how a single decision can literally mean the difference between life and death.

For many, this story reinforces the idea that we should cherish every moment and treat each interaction with kindness, as we never know how it might affect our lives or the lives of others. It's a tale that continues to resonate, prompting reflection on the nature of fate, the butterfly effect of our decisions, and the profound interconnectedness of human lives.

Chapter Thirty-Five

The Time Capsule Coincidence: A Bridge Across Decades

In 2007, a small town in Middle America experienced an extraordinary coincidence that seemed to bridge the gap between past and present in an almost poetic manner. This is the story of a time capsule, buried in 1957, that created an unexpected connection across generations.

The event took place during the town's centennial celebrations. As part of the festivities, city officials decided to unearth a time capsule that had been buried 50 years earlier during the town's 50th anniversary. The capsule, a sturdy metal box, had been filled with items meant to represent life in 1957 and sealed with instructions to be opened in 2007.

As the capsule was opened in front of an eager crowd, city officials began to remove and display its contents. There were newspapers, photographs, and various artifacts from 1957. But one item, in particular, caught everyone's attention - a copy of the local magazine from 1957.

The magazine featured an article about a local teenager who had won a science fair with an innovative project. The article praised the young scientist's potential and speculated about the bright future ahead of him. It was a typical piece celebrating local talent, the kind often found in small-town publications.

What made this article extraordinary was the presence of its subject at the time capsule opening ceremony. The teenager from the 1957 article, now an elderly man, was in attendance. He had gone on to have a successful career as a scientist, fulfilling the potential noted in the article half a century earlier.

The man, who had long forgotten about the article, was visibly moved when he saw his younger self staring back at him from the yellowed pages of the magazine. It was as if his past and present had suddenly collided in a tangible way.

This coincidence captivated the town. The chance that the subject of an article in a 50-year-old time capsule would be present at its opening seemed incredibly small. It provided a powerful visual representation of the passage of time and the fulfillment of potential.

The event sparked discussions about legacy, the passage of time, and the unpredictable nature of life. Many saw it as a reminder of how our actions in the present can echo into the future in ways we can't foresee.

For the man himself, it was a profound moment of reflection. Seeing the hopes and expectations placed on him as a teenager, and knowing the path his life had taken since, brought a sense of accomplishment and nostalgia.

This time capsule coincidence serves as a heartwarming reminder of the connections that can span decades. It highlights how artifacts from the past can suddenly become relevant in unexpected ways, creating moments of serendipity that touch our lives and our communities.

Chapter Thirty-Six

The Preemptive Eulogy: Mark Twain's Premature Obituary

Mark Twain, the celebrated American author and humorist, was known for his wit and his ability to find humor in almost any situation. In 1897, he found himself at the center of a coincidence that would give birth to one of his most famous quips and highlight the sometimes premature nature of obituaries.

The incident began when Twain's cousin, who had been seriously ill, passed away. Somehow, in the process of reporting this death, a rumor began to circulate that it was Mark Twain himself who had died. The rumor quickly gained traction and made its way to New York.

A reporter from the New York Journal, eager to get the scoop on such a significant story, was dispatched to investigate. The reporter cabled Twain's London address, seeking confirmation of the author's demise.

Twain, very much alive and characteristically amused by the situation, responded with what would become one of his most famous quotes: "The reports of my death are greatly exaggerated."

This witty response not only put to rest the rumors of his death but also showcased Twain's quick wit and humor in the face of such a bizarre situation. The incident quickly became a topic of amusement in literary circles and among Twain's fans.

What makes this situation particularly coincidental is that it stemmed from the actual death of Twain's cousin. The mix-up in identities, the speed at which the false information spread, and Twain's fortuitous presence in London to receive and respond to the inquiry all combined to create this memorable moment.

The incident highlights the sometimes unreliable nature of news reporting, especially in an era before instant global communication. It also serves as a reminder of how easily misinformation can spread and the importance of fact-checking.

For Twain, this premature obituary became a part of his legend. He would go on to reference it multiple times in his writings and speeches, always with his characteristic humor. In fact, Twain lived for another 13 years after this incident, passing away in 1910.

This coincidence has since become a favorite anecdote among literary enthusiasts and is often cited as an example of Twain's quick wit. It also serves as a cautionary tale in journalism about the dangers of rushing to report news without proper verification.

The preemptive eulogy of Mark Twain stands as a testament to the author's humor and the strange ways in which fact and fiction can sometimes intertwine. It remains one of the most famous incidents of a premature obituary, a peculiar honor that seemed perfectly suited to a man of Twain's unique character and wit.

Chapter Thirty-Seven

The Winning Lottery Ticket: A Wash Day Miracle

In 2005, a remarkable story emerged from Uncasville, Connecticut, that seemed to defy all odds and gave new meaning to the phrase "laundering money". This tale of luck, forgetfulness, and an incredibly resilient lottery ticket captivated the public and became a testament to the unpredictable nature of fortune.

The story centers around Joanne Hubbard, a grandmother from Uncasville. Like many people, Joanne occasionally bought lottery tickets, dreaming of the chance to win big. One day, she purchased a ticket for the Connecticut Powerball drawing, tucked it into her pocket, and went about her day.

What happened next was a sequence of events that could have easily led to disaster but instead resulted in an astonishing stroke of luck. Joanne forgot about the ticket in her pocket and did her laundry. The lottery ticket went through a full wash cycle, emerging as a soggy, illegible mess.

It was only later, when the winning numbers were announced, that Joanne remembered her ticket. To her shock and dismay, she realized that her numbers matched the winning combination. The potential prize was a staggering $869,000. But there was a problem - the ticket was now a waterlogged, unreadable scrap of paper.

Most people would have given up at this point, assuming that a washed lottery ticket would be invalid. But Joanne decided to take a chance. She contacted the Connecticut Lottery Corporation and explained her situation.

In an unprecedented move, lottery officials agreed to try to salvage the ticket. They worked with lottery experts and even a forensics team to piece together the remains of the ticket and verify its authenticity. After careful examination and reconstruction, they were able to confirm that it was indeed the winning ticket.

Against all odds, Joanne was awarded her prize of $869,000. The story made headlines across the country, with many amazed at both Joanne's luck in winning and the extraordinary circumstances that followed.

This incident serves as a reminder of how close we can come to missing out on life-changing opportunities. It highlights the importance of perseverance and the sometimes miraculous ways in which things can work out.

The tale of the washed lottery ticket has since become a favorite among those who love stories of incredible coincidences and near-misses. It's often recounted as an example of how fortune can smile on us in the most unexpected ways, even when all seems lost.

For lottery players everywhere, it became a cautionary tale about keeping track of tickets, but also a source of hope that even in the most unlikely circumstances, luck can prevail. The incident even led some lottery organizations to review their policies regarding damaged tickets.

Joanne Hubbard's wash day miracle remains one of the most extraordinary lottery stories ever told, a true testament to the unpredictable nature of luck and the resilience of both paper and human spirit.

Chapter Thirty-Eight

The Titanic Survivor's Book: A Prophetic Tale

In the realm of coincidences, few stories are as chilling and prophetic as that of the Titanic survivor who carried with him a book that seemed to foretell the very disaster he would soon experience. This tale, which blurs the lines between fiction and reality, centers around a passenger named William Thomas Stead.

William Stead was a prominent British journalist and editor who boarded the Titanic for its maiden voyage in April 1912. Among his belongings was a book titled "Futility, or the Wreck of the Titan," written by Morgan Robertson and published in 1898 – 14 years before the Titanic's ill-fated journey.

The eerie parallels between Robertson's fictional story and the real-life Titanic disaster are numerous and uncanny:

1. In the book, the ship was named "Titan," strikingly similar to "Titanic."

2. Both the fictional Titan and the real Titanic were described as the largest ships of their time.

3. Both were considered unsinkable.

4. Both did not have enough lifeboats for all passengers.

5. Both struck an iceberg in the North Atlantic in April.

6. Both sank, resulting in massive loss of life.

The similarities were so striking that after the Titanic disaster, many people accused Robertson of clairvoyance or some form of precognition.

What makes this coincidence even more remarkable is that Stead, carrying this prophetic book, was himself a passenger on the Titanic. He did not survive the sinking, adding another layer of tragedy and irony to the tale.

Stead was known for his interest in spiritualism and the paranormal, which made his possession of this seemingly prophetic book all the more intriguing to many. Some speculated that he might have sensed the impending doom, though there's no evidence to support this.

This extraordinary coincidence has fascinated people for decades. It raises questions about the nature of prediction, the thin line between fiction and reality, and the sometimes uncanny ways in which art can seem to anticipate life.

Skeptics point out that there were also many differences between the book and the real event, and that given the number of stories written about shipwrecks, some coincidences were bound to occur. Nevertheless, the parallels remain striking.

The story of William Stead and his prophetic book has become a part of Titanic lore, often recounted as one of the most bizarre coincidences surrounding the tragic event. It serves as a reminder of the unpredictable nature of fate and the sometimes eerie ways in which fiction can mirror reality.

This tale continues to captivate those interested in the Titanic disaster, as well as enthusiasts of strange coincidences and apparent premonitions. It stands as a testament to the enduring human fascination with the mysterious and the seemingly inexplicable.

Chapter Thirty-Nine

The Coincidental Car Crash: Twin Brothers' Unexpected Reunion

In the realm of improbable events, the story of the coincidental car crash that occurred in 2002 in Finland stands out as a truly remarkable tale. This incident not only defied odds but also brought about an unexpected family reunion in the most dramatic of circumstances.

The event took place on a seemingly ordinary day on a highway in northern Finland. Two cars collided in a head-on crash. Fortunately, the collision was not severe, and both drivers escaped with only minor injuries. However, what happened next turned this routine traffic accident into an extraordinary coincidence.

As the two drivers emerged from their vehicles to assess the damage and exchange information, they were struck by an uncanny resemblance to each other. Upon closer inspection and conversation, they made a startling discovery – they were identical twin brothers, separated at birth and unaware of each other's existence for 39 years.

The brothers, whose names were not disclosed to protect their privacy, had been born in 1963. Due to circumstances unknown to them, they were separated as infants and adopted by different families. Neither knew of the other's existence, and their adoptive families had never told them they had a twin.

By an incredible twist of fate, both brothers had ended up living in the same region of Finland. They had gone about their lives for nearly four decades, unaware that they had an identical twin living nearby. It took this chance encounter – a minor car crash – to bring them face to face.

The odds of such an event occurring are astronomically low. For twin brothers, separated at birth, to not only live in the same area but also to literally crash into each other, seems almost too coincidental to be true. Yet, this is exactly what happened.

This extraordinary meeting led to a flurry of emotions and questions for the brothers. They spent hours talking at the crash site, piecing together their separate but parallel lives. The incident sparked a journey of discovery as they delved into their past, seeking answers about their birth and separation.

The story quickly captured media attention in Finland and soon spread internationally. It fascinated the public and experts alike, becoming a topic of discussion in psychology circles about the nature vs. nurture debate and the bonds between twins.

This coincidental car crash serves as a powerful reminder of the unpredictable nature of life and the strange ways in which destinies can intersect. It highlights how seemingly random events can lead to life-changing discoveries and reunions.

The tale of these twin brothers continues to be recounted as one of the most extraordinary coincidences in recent history. It stands as a testament to the sometimes inexplicable workings of fate and the enduring connections that can exist between siblings, even when separated by time and circumstance.

Chapter Forty

The Bullet-Stopping Bible: A Soldier's Miraculous Escape

In the annals of wartime miracles, few stories are as compelling and widely circulated as that of the bullet-stopping Bible. This extraordinary event, which occurred during World War I, serves as a powerful testament to both chance and faith, captivating both believers and skeptics alike.

The incident took place in 1914, during the early months of World War I. A British soldier, whose name has been recorded as Private Elmer Hildreth, was serving on the Western Front. Like many soldiers, Hildreth carried a small Bible in his breast pocket, a common practice that provided both spiritual comfort and a connection to home.

During a particularly fierce battle, Hildreth's unit came under heavy fire. In the chaos of combat, a German bullet struck the young soldier directly in the chest, right where his heart was located. By all accounts, it should have been a fatal shot.

However, when Hildreth checked himself for injuries, he found that the bullet had not penetrated his body. Upon investigation, he discovered that the bullet had struck the small Bible in his breast pocket. The book had absorbed the impact of the bullet, stopping it from reaching Hildreth's heart.

Upon closer examination, it was found that the bullet had penetrated partway through the Bible, coming to rest at the Book of Psalms. Specifically, it had stopped at Psalm 91, which reads in part: "A thousand may fall at your side, ten thousand at your right hand, but it will not come near you."

The incident was seen by many as nothing short of miraculous. The odds of a small book stopping a high-velocity bullet are incredibly low, and the fact that it stopped at such a pertinent passage added another layer of astonishment to the event.

News of Hildreth's miraculous escape spread quickly among the troops and eventually made its way back home. The story was published in newspapers, bolstering morale and providing a ray of hope amidst the darkest days of the war.

This tale of the bullet-stopping Bible has since become a part of World War I folklore. It has been recounted in numerous books about wartime coincidences and miracles, and similar stories have emerged from other conflicts.

For many, this incident serves as a powerful affirmation of faith, a tangible example of divine protection. For others, it's a remarkable coincidence that highlights the sometimes random nature of survival in warfare.

Regardless of one's personal beliefs, the story of the bullet-stopping Bible remains a compelling tale of survival against the odds. It continues to fascinate people today, serving as a reminder of the thin line between life and death in wartime, and the sometimes inexplicable nature of fortune in the face of danger.

Chapter Forty-One

The Recurring Dream Number: A Lottery Winner's Premonition

In the world of lottery wins, there are countless stories of lucky guesses and random selections leading to fortune. However, few are as intriguing as the tale of a man whose recurring dream led him to a life-changing lottery win. This story, which blurs the line between coincidence and premonition, has fascinated many since its occurrence.

The protagonist of this extraordinary tale is a man from the Midwestern United States (his name is often withheld in retellings to protect his privacy). For three consecutive nights, this man had a vivid and unusual dream. In each dream, he saw the same four-digit number: 7316. The number seemed to have no particular significance to him, and he had no idea why it kept appearing in his dreams.

After the third night of dreaming about this number, the man decided that perhaps there was more to it than just a random figment of his subconscious. On a whim, he decided to play the number in his state's daily lottery game.

To his astonishment, the number 7316 was drawn as the winning number that day. The man's decision to act on his recurring dream had led him to win a substantial prize in the lottery.

This story quickly captured public imagination when it was reported. Many were fascinated by the idea that a dream could predict a real-world outcome, especially one as unpredictable as a lottery draw. The incident sparked discussions about precognition, the nature of dreams, and the potential for subconscious information processing.

Skeptics, of course, point out that coincidences like this are bound to happen given the millions of lottery tickets purchased daily and the common occurrence of number dreams. They argue that we only hear about the hits and not the countless misses where dream numbers don't pan out.

However, for many, the specificity of the number and its recurrence over three nights, followed by an immediate win, seems to go beyond mere chance. Some see it as evidence of extrasensory perception or a momentary glimpse into the future.

Psychologists and dream researchers have also weighed in on the phenomenon. Some suggest that our brains are constantly processing information, even when we sleep, and that sometimes this can lead to insights or pattern recognition that we're not consciously aware of.

Regardless of how one interprets it, the story of the recurring dream number serves as a captivating example of the mysterious ways in which our minds can sometimes seem to connect with future events. It continues to be cited in discussions about the nature of coincidence, the potential meanings of dreams, and the unpredictable nature of luck.

For the lottery winner himself, whether it was extraordinary luck or something more mystical, the experience certainly proved to be life-changing. His story remains a favorite among those who love tales of dreams coming true in the most literal and fortunate of ways.

Chapter Forty-Two

The Prophetic Homework: A Student's Uncanny Prediction

In the realm of historical coincidences, few stories are as intriguing as the tale of a Swedish student's remarkably accurate prediction of future events. This incident, which occurred in 1958, stands as a testament to the sometimes uncanny accuracy of human foresight and the unpredictable nature of historical change.

The story begins in a classroom in Stockholm, Sweden. A history professor, intrigued by the rapid pace of technological and social change in the post-war era, assigned his students an unusual task. They were to write essays predicting what they thought the world would be like in 30 years' time – in 1988.

Most students produced fairly conventional predictions, extrapolating from current trends of the late 1950s. However, one student's essay stood out for its startlingly accurate forecasts. This student, whose name has been lost to history, made a series of predictions that would prove to be remarkably prescient.

Among the student's predictions was one that was particularly striking: the fall of the Berlin Wall. The student wrote that by 1988, the division between East and West Germany would become untenable, and that the Berlin Wall would be dismantled.

At the time, this prediction seemed far-fetched. The Berlin Wall had not even been built when the essay was written – its construction would not begin until 1961. The Cold War was at its height, and the division of Germany seemed a permanent fixture of the global political landscape.

Yet, as history unfolded, the student's prediction proved to be uncannily accurate. While the timing was slightly off – the Berlin Wall fell in 1989 rather than 1988 – the essence of the prediction was spot on. The seemingly impregnable barrier between East and West did indeed come down, marking the end of the Cold War era.

When this essay was rediscovered in the late 1980s, it caused a sensation. Many were amazed at the student's foresight, wondering how a young person in the 1950s could have so accurately predicted such a momentous event.

Some speculated that the student must have had insider knowledge or exceptional political insight. Others saw it as a lucky guess – a shot in the dark that happened to hit the mark. Still others viewed it as evidence of the human mind's capacity for extrapolation and prediction.

Regardless of how one interprets it, this incident serves as a fascinating example of historical foresight. It reminds us that even in times of apparent stability, the seeds of great change are often already present, waiting to be recognized by those with the vision to see them.

The story of the prophetic homework continues to intrigue historians and futurists alike. It stands as a testament to the power of imagination and the sometimes surprising accuracy of human prediction, even in the face of seemingly unchangeable historical circumstances.

Last edited 46 minutes ago

Chapter Forty-Three

The Coincidental Car Colors: A Parking Lot Surprise

In the world of automotive coincidences, few stories are as visually striking as the tale of the matching cars that unfolded in a Detroit parking lot in 1975. This incident, while simple in nature, serves as a delightful example of how random chance can sometimes create moments of perfect symmetry in our everyday lives.

The story begins on an ordinary day in Detroit, Michigan, a city known for its deep connections to the automotive industry. A man, whose name has been lost to history, drove his car to a local shopping center. He parked his vehicle – a brand new, bright yellow Ford Pinto – and went about his shopping.

When he returned to the parking lot, he was met with an astonishing sight. Parked directly behind his yellow Pinto was another car – identical in make, model, and color. Two bright yellow Ford Pintos, side by side in a sea of more neutral-colored vehicles.

Amazed by this coincidence, the man decided to wait and see who the owner of the other Pinto might be. As he waited, he noticed something even more extraordinary. The license plates of the two cars were sequential. His own plate ended in 494, while the plate on the other Pinto ended in 495.

The odds of two identical cars, in a distinctive color, with consecutive license plate numbers, parking next to each other by chance are astronomically low. Yet here it was, a perfect alignment of coincidences creating a memorable visual spectacle.

When the owner of the other Pinto returned, the two men were equally amazed by the situation. They discovered that they had purchased their cars from different dealerships on different days. The consecutive license plates were purely a result of chance in the state's plate assignment system.

This incident quickly became a talking point in the local community. Many saw it as a delightful example of life's unexpected surprises. Others viewed it as a strange alignment of probabilities, a reminder of how even the most unlikely events can sometimes occur.

The story of the matching Pintos serves as a charming reminder of how coincidences can bring a touch of wonder to our everyday lives. It highlights the joy that can be found in noticing and appreciating these small, unlikely occurrences.

In a broader sense, this incident speaks to our human tendency to find patterns and meaning in random events. It's a trait that has driven scientific discovery and artistic creation throughout human history.

While not as profound as some historical coincidences, the tale of the matching Pintos continues to be shared as a lighthearted example of life's unexpected symmetries. It stands as a testament to the small wonders that can occur when chance aligns just right, creating moments of surprise and delight in the most ordinary of settings.

Chapter Forty-Four

The Doppelgänger Photo: A Party Surprise

In the age of social media and ubiquitous photography, the chances of discovering your doppelgänger – a person who looks remarkably similar to you – have increased dramatically. However, few stories of doppelgänger discoveries are as striking as the incident that occurred in Ireland in 2015, which came to be known as "The Doppelgänger Photo."

The story begins with a man named Neil Douglas, a resident of Glasgow, Scotland. Neil was attending a friend's wedding in Galway, Ireland, and as part of the festivities, he posed for numerous photos with other guests. It was a typical wedding celebration, with nothing out of the ordinary – until Neil's friend showed him one particular photo from the event.

In this photo, Neil saw himself – or so he thought at first glance. Upon closer inspection, he realized that the man in the photo, while bearing an uncanny resemblance to himself, was actually a stranger. The man had the same beard, hairstyle, and even similar facial features. The resemblance was so striking that it was hard to tell them apart.

Intrigued and somewhat amazed, Neil decided to track down his looka-like. Through mutual friends and social media, he managed to identify the man as Robert Stirling, another wedding guest who lived in London.

What makes this story even more remarkable is that Neil and Robert had never met before the wedding. They were not related, had grown up in different countries, and had led entirely separate lives. Yet, by some strange twist of genetic fate, they looked almost identical.

The story of Neil and Robert's doppelgänger discovery quickly went viral on social media. Many were fascinated by the uncanny resemblance between two unrelated individuals. The photo of Neil and Robert side by side, both sporting the same beard and hairstyle, became an internet sensation.

This incident sparked discussions about genetics, probability, and the concept of doppelgängers. Scientists explain that while it's rare to find an exact lookalike, it's not impossible given the finite combinations of human features and the vast global population.

For Neil and Robert, this coincidence led to an unexpected friendship. They stayed in touch after the wedding, bonding over their shared appearance and the unusual circumstances of their meeting. Their story has been featured in numerous news articles and television segments, making them minor celebrities in the world of remarkable coincidences.

The tale of "The Doppelgänger Photo" serves as a delightful reminder of the surprises that life can offer. It highlights how in our interconnected world, we might be closer to our lookalike than we think. It also underscores the joy and wonder that can come from embracing these strange coincidences when they occur.

This story continues to fascinate people, serving as a modern-day example of truth being stranger than fiction. It stands as a testament to the unpredictable nature of genetics and the sometimes extraordinary outcomes of chance encounters.

Chapter Forty-Five

The Lottery Prediction: A Psychic's Lucky Guess

In the world of psychic predictions and lottery wins, few stories are as remarkable as the incident that occurred in Australia in 1986. This event, which saw a woman correctly predict the winning lottery numbers just a day before the draw, has since become a fascinating case study in the realms of precognition and probability.

The protagonist of this extraordinary tale was Maureen Summers, a self-proclaimed psychic from Melbourne, Australia. Summers had gained some local fame for her alleged ability to predict future events, but what happened on August 22, 1986, would catapult her into national spotlight.

On that day, Summers was interviewed by a local newspaper about her psychic abilities. During the interview, the topic of the upcoming Saturday lotto draw came up. To the journalist's surprise, Summers confidently stated that she knew what the winning numbers would be. When pressed, she wrote down six numbers on a piece of paper, sealed it in an envelope, and handed it to the journalist.

The next day, August 23, the lotto numbers were drawn. To the astonishment of everyone involved, the numbers matched exactly those that Summers had predicted and sealed in the envelope just 24 hours earlier.

The odds of correctly guessing all six numbers in a lotto draw are astronomical - typically in the millions to one. For Summers to have done this, and to have done so in such a public and verifiable manner, seemed to defy all probability.

News of Summers' prediction spread rapidly across Australia and soon made international headlines. Many saw it as compelling evidence of psychic abilities, while skeptics searched for alternative explanations. Some suggested that Summers might have had inside information about the draw, though investigations found no evidence of this.

The incident sparked intense debate in both scientific and paranormal circles. Parapsychologists saw it as a potential breakthrough in proving the existence of precognition. Statisticians and skeptics, on the other hand, pointed out that given the number of psychics making predictions and the frequency of lottery draws, occasional correct guesses, while improbable, are not impossible.

For Summers herself, the correct prediction brought both fame and scrutiny. She maintained that her abilities were genuine, but was unable to replicate her success in subsequent lottery predictions.

This case remains one of the most well-documented instances of an apparently successful prediction of random future events. It continues to be discussed in books and articles about psychic phenomena and the nature of probability.

The lottery prediction incident serves as a fascinating example of the fine line between incredible coincidence and seemingly inexplicable foresight. It reminds us of the complex relationship between chance, probability, and our human desire to find meaning and pattern in random events.

Chapter Forty-Six

The Prophetic Nickname: Joseph Beuys' Fateful Moniker

In the annals of artistic lore, few stories are as intriguing and seemingly prophetic as that of Joseph Beuys, the influential German artist known for his sculptures, performances, and installations. His life story, particularly the origin of his childhood nickname and its connection to his later experiences, presents a coincidence that borders on the mythical.

Joseph Beuys was born in 1921 in Krefeld, Germany. As a child, he was given the nickname "Jup" by his friends. This simple, affectionate moniker seemed unremarkable at the time, just another playground nickname. However, its significance would only become apparent years later, in the midst of World War II.

During the war, Beuys served as a radio operator and rear gunner in the Luftwaffe. In 1944, his plane was shot down over the Crimean Front. This is where the story takes an extraordinary turn, one that would shape both Beuys' life and his artistic career.

According to Beuys' own account, he was found unconscious by a group of nomadic Tatar tribesmen. These people, he claimed, saved his life by covering his body in animal fat and wrapping him in felt to keep him warm. They also fed him honey and cheese during his recovery.

The connection to his childhood nickname "Jup" becomes apparent when one considers that "Jup" is phonetically similar to the German word "Fett," meaning "fat." Moreover, felt and fat became central materials in Beuys' later artistic work, featuring prominently in many of his most famous pieces.

The coincidence of Beuys' childhood nickname predicting the very materials that would not only reportedly save his life but also define his artistic career is truly remarkable. It's as if his destiny was somehow encoded in this simple childhood appellation.

This story, combining elements of biography, artistic mythology, and seeming predestination, has fascinated art historians and coincidence enthusiasts alike. Some view it as a powerful example of how early life experiences can shape an artist's work in unexpected ways. Others see it as a carefully crafted narrative, part of Beuys' artistic persona.

Regardless of one's interpretation, the tale of Joseph Beuys' prophetic nickname serves as a captivating example of how seemingly insignificant details from our past can take on profound significance in light of later events. It underscores the human tendency to find meaning and connection in the disparate elements of our lives, weaving them into a coherent narrative.

In the end, whether viewed as coincidence, destiny, or artistic mythmaking, the story of Beuys' nickname remains a powerful part of his legacy. It continues to intrigue and inspire, reminding us of the sometimes mysterious ways in which our lives unfold and the unexpected connections that can emerge between our past and our future.

Chapter Forty-Seven

The Life-Saving Bet: A Wager with Destiny

In the realm of life-and-death coincidences, few stories are as poignant and thought-provoking as the tale of the life-saving bet that occurred in 1973. This extraordinary event, which saw a man's playful wager with his wife inadvertently save his life, serves as a powerful reminder of the unpredictable nature of existence and the sometimes razor-thin line between life and death.

The story begins with a middle-aged couple from Birmingham, England. The husband, whose name has been withheld in most retellings to protect his privacy, had been experiencing some health issues. His wife, concerned about his wellbeing, had been urging him to take better care of himself and to see a doctor for a thorough check-up.

In a moment of levity, possibly to ease the tension surrounding his health concerns, the husband made a bet with his wife. He wagered that he could live for one more year without any major health incidents. The prize? If he won, his wife would have to cook his favorite meal every day for a month.

What started as a lighthearted bet took on a more serious tone as the year progressed. The husband, perhaps motivated by the wager, indeed took better care of his health. He improved his diet, started exercising more regularly, and even went for the medical check-up his wife had been advocating.

As the one-year mark approached, the couple's anticipation grew. Then, on the exact day the bet was set to conclude, the unthinkable happened. The husband suffered a massive heart attack.

Remarkably, because of the improved lifestyle changes he had made over the past year and the recent medical check-up that had caught some early warning signs, the husband survived the heart attack. Doctors later confirmed that had he not made these changes, the outcome would likely have been fatal.

The irony of the situation was not lost on the couple. What had started as a playful bet had literally saved the husband's life. The wager had motivated him to make the very changes that allowed him to survive a potentially lethal health crisis.

This incident quickly became a talking point among their friends and family, eventually catching the attention of local media. Many saw it as a powerful example of how small decisions and seemingly inconsequential actions can have life-altering consequences.

The story of the life-saving bet serves as a poignant reminder of the unpredictable nature of life and death. It highlights how our choices, even those made in jest, can have profound impacts on our futures. It also underscores the importance of preventive health care and the potential life-saving benefits of regular check-ups and lifestyle improvements.

For the couple involved, this extraordinary coincidence became a defining moment in their lives, a testament to the power of love, humor, and perhaps a touch of fate in the face of life's uncertainties. Their story continues to be shared as an inspiring example of how a simple bet can sometimes turn into a wager with destiny itself.

Chapter Forty-Eight

The Recurring Death Date: A Family's Eerie Pattern

In the tapestry of family histories, patterns often emerge - shared traits, common professions, or recurring names. But for one family in New Delhi, India, a far more unsettling pattern came to light, one that spanned generations and defied rational explanation. This is the story of the recurring death date, a coincidence so extraordinary that it captured the attention of statisticians and paranormal researchers alike.

The story begins with a discovery made by the family in the early 2000s. While reviewing their family history, they noticed a chilling pattern: for three consecutive generations, a male member of the family had died on June 7th, all at the age of 57.

The first recorded incident was the death of the family patriarch on June 7th, 1967, at the age of 57. Exactly 19 years later, on June 7th, 1986, his son also passed away, having just turned 57 a few months prior. The pattern continued into the third generation when, on June 7th, 2005, the grandson died, also at the age of 57.

The odds of such a specific pattern occurring by chance are astronomically low. Not only did these deaths occur on the same date across three generations, but they also happened at the same age. This level of specificity went beyond what most would consider a mere coincidence.

When this pattern came to light, it understandably caused great distress within the family. Male members approaching their late 50s began to view the date of June 7th with a sense of dread. Some family members sought explanations in genetics, wondering if there might be a hereditary condition that manifested fatally at this specific age.

Others looked to more mystical explanations, considering concepts like family curses or karmic patterns. The story attracted the attention of parapsychologists and researchers interested in anomalous phenomena, who saw it as a potential case study in patterns that seemed to defy conventional explanation.

Statisticians, while acknowledging the extraordinary nature of the coincidence, cautioned against reading too much into it. They pointed out that given the vast number of families and the countless possibilities for patterns to emerge, some families would inevitably experience seemingly impossible coincidences.

Regardless of the explanation, the impact on the family was profound. Some members chose to undergo extensive medical testing as they approached the age of 57, while others made significant life changes, determined to break the pattern.

This case of the recurring death date serves as a fascinating example of how patterns can emerge in family histories, sometimes in ways that seem to defy probability. It highlights our human tendency to seek meaning in coincidences and the powerful impact that perceived patterns can have on our psyche and behavior.

Whether viewed as a statistical anomaly, a quirk of fate, or something more mysterious, the story of this family's recurring death date continues to intrigue those who hear it. It stands as a testament to the complex and sometimes inexplicable ways in which our lives and deaths can align, creating patterns that challenge our understanding of chance and destiny.

Chapter Forty-Nine

The Identical Bank Robbers: A Case of Mistaken Identity

In the annals of criminal justice, few cases are as perplexing and coincidental as the story of the identical bank robbers that unfolded in Ohio in 2008. This extraordinary event not only highlighted the challenges faced by law enforcement but also raised intriguing questions about genetics and behavior.

The incident began when a bank in Columbus, Ohio, was robbed by a man who managed to escape with a significant amount of cash. Security cameras captured clear images of the perpetrator, and police quickly began their search based on this evidence.

Within days, law enforcement officials believed they had their man. They arrested a suspect who matched the description and bore an uncanny resemblance to the individual in the security footage. The man vehemently proclaimed his innocence, providing an alibi for the time of the robbery. However, given the striking similarity to the suspect in the video, police were skeptical of his claims.

As the investigation progressed, a startling discovery was made. The arrested man had an identical twin brother. When police located and questioned the brother, they were stunned to find that he was an exact match for both the man in custody and the individual in the security footage.

Further investigation revealed that it was, in fact, the twin brother who had committed the robbery. The arrested man had been telling the truth about his innocence all along. The real perpetrator had been leveraging their identical appearance, perhaps counting on the confusion it would cause if he were caught.

This case presented a unique challenge for the justice system. The physical evidence - primarily the security camera footage - was rendered almost useless due to the identical appearance of the twins. It became crucial to establish solid alibis and gather other forms of evidence to determine which twin was actually responsible for the crime.

The incident sparked discussions in legal and scientific circles about the challenges posed by identical twins in criminal investigations. It highlighted the limitations of eyewitness testimony and even some forms of physical evidence when dealing with genetically identical individuals.

For the wrongly accused twin, the experience was a harrowing ordeal. Despite his innocence, he had been arrested and held based on his appearance alone. His story served as a cautionary tale about the potential pitfalls of relying too heavily on visual identification in criminal cases.

This case of the identical bank robbers remains a fascinating example of how genetic similarity can complicate criminal investigations. It serves as a reminder of the importance of thorough investigation and the potential for extraordinary coincidences to impact the pursuit of justice.

The story continues to be cited in discussions about the reliability of eyewitness testimony, the challenges of forensic evidence, and the unique legal and ethical questions raised by cases involving identical twins. It stands as a testament to the complex interplay between genetics, identity, and the criminal justice system.

Chapter Fifty

The Prophetic License Plate: A Life-Saving Coincidence

In the realm of meaningful coincidences, few stories are as powerful and life-affirming as the tale of the prophetic license plate. This extraordinary event, which occurred in California, serves as a testament to the sometimes inexplicable connections between seemingly random occurrences and life-altering moments.

The story centers around a man from San Diego, California. When he first received his car registration, he was assigned a seemingly random license plate number. The plate contained his initials followed by "THX" - a common abbreviation for "thanks." At the time, he thought nothing of it, considering it a pleasant but unremarkable coincidence that his initials were included.

Years passed, and the man went about his life, his unique license plate a minor footnote in his daily existence. However, this mundane detail would soon take on an incredible significance.

In his mid-40s, the man was diagnosed with a severe kidney disease. His condition deteriorated rapidly, and it became clear that he would need a kidney transplant to survive. He was placed on the transplant waiting list, joining thousands of others in a race against time.

Months of anxious waiting followed, with regular dialysis treatments becoming a central part of his life. Then, one day, he received the call he had been desperately hoping for - a matching kidney had been found, and he was scheduled for immediate transplant surgery.

The surgery was successful, and as the man recovered, he was filled with gratitude for his anonymous donor. It was only when he inquired about the possibility of thanking his donor's family that the true magnitude of the coincidence was revealed.

He learned that his kidney donor's initials were T.H.X. - the exact letters that followed his initials on his license plate. The plate he had been carrying for years had, in a sense, predicted the very thing that would save his life.

This extraordinary coincidence left the man and his doctors astounded. The odds of receiving a kidney from a donor whose initials matched the letters on his license plate were incredibly small. Many saw it as more than mere chance - perhaps a sign of some greater design or cosmic connection.

The story quickly spread, capturing the imagination of local media and then gaining national attention. It resonated with many people, especially those who had experienced or were waiting for organ transplants. For them, it was a story of hope and the mysterious workings of fate.

This case of the prophetic license plate serves as a powerful reminder of the unexpected ways in which our lives can be touched by seeming coincidences. It highlights the profound impact that organ donation can have and the sometimes inexplicable connections that can exist between donor and recipient.

The man's story continues to be shared as an inspiring example of serendipity and the potential for meaning in the seemingly random details of our lives. It stands as a testament to the complex tapestry of chance and circumstance that shapes human experience, reminding us that sometimes, the most mundane details can foreshadow life's most significant moments.

Chapter Fifty-One

The Recurring Taxi Number: A Week of Unlikely Encounters

In the bustling metropolis of London, where thousands of black cabs crisscross the city daily, one woman experienced a week of coincidences so improbable that it defies conventional explanation. This is the story of the recurring taxi number, a tale that challenges our understanding of chance and probability.

The incident began on a Monday morning when a woman, let's call her Sarah, hailed a taxi to take her to work. As she settled into the back seat, she absently noted the taxi's license number. Little did she know that this mundane detail would become the start of an extraordinary week.

The next day, Tuesday, Sarah again took a taxi to work. To her surprise, she realized that the cab had the exact same license number as the one from the previous day. Amused by the coincidence, she mentioned it to the driver, who was equally surprised.

On Wednesday, lightning struck a third time. Once again, Sarah found herself in a taxi with the same license number. By this point, she was beginning to feel a mixture of amazement and unease. The odds of randomly hailing the same taxi three days in a row in a city the size of London are astronomically low.

As the week progressed, the pattern continued. Thursday, Friday, Saturday - each day, Sarah encountered a taxi with the same license number. She began to wonder if she was experiencing some sort of elaborate prank or if there was a glitch in the matrix of reality.

By Sunday, the final day of this extraordinary week, Sarah had become both fascinated and slightly unnerved by the recurring taxi number. Half-expecting it, half-dreading it, she hailed a cab for a trip across town. Sure enough, it bore the now-familiar license number.

In a finale that seemed almost scripted, Sarah decided to engage the driver in conversation about this strange occurrence. To her astonishment, the driver revealed that this was, in fact, his taxi - the very same vehicle she had been riding in all week. He explained that he had recently changed his route and schedule, which had led to this improbable series of encounters.

This revelation brought a sense of closure to Sarah's week of coincidences. While it explained the recurring number, it did little to diminish the extraordinary nature of the experience. The odds of repeatedly encountering the same taxi in London, even with the driver's changed route, remain incredibly small.

Sarah's story quickly spread among her friends and colleagues, eventually catching the attention of local media. It sparked discussions about probability, the nature of coincidence, and whether such sequences of events could truly be random.

For many, the tale of the recurring taxi number serves as a fascinating example of how seemingly impossible coincidences can occur in everyday life. It reminds us that in a world of countless interactions and possibilities, even the most unlikely events can sometimes unfold.

This story continues to intrigue those who hear it, standing as a testament to the unpredictable and sometimes inexplicable nature of our daily experiences. It challenges us to remain open to the extraordinary possibilities that might be hiding within the seemingly ordinary fabric of our lives.

Chapter Fifty-Two

The Simultaneous Inventions: Bell and Gray's Telephone Coincidence

In the annals of scientific history, few coincidences are as striking or as consequential as the simultaneous invention of the telephone by Alexander Graham Bell and Elisha Gray. This extraordinary event, which occurred on February 14, 1876, not only shaped the course of communication technology but also led to one of the most famous patent disputes in history.

The story begins with two inventors working independently on similar ideas. Alexander Graham Bell, a Scottish-born scientist and inventor, had been experimenting with ways to transmit speech electrically. Meanwhile, Elisha Gray, an American electrical engineer, was working on a similar concept.

On that fateful Valentine's Day in 1876, both men separately filed for patents related to the telephone. Bell's lawyer filed his patent application at the U.S. Patent Office in Washington, D.C., just a few hours before Gray's lawyer arrived to file a caveat (a type of preliminary patent document) for a similar device.

The coincidence of timing was remarkable. Two men, working independently and unaware of each other's progress, had not only developed similar inventions but had also chosen to file their patent documents on the exact same day. The margin of difference in their filing times was mere hours.

This coincidence led to a protracted legal battle over the rights to the telephone patent. Bell was ultimately awarded the patent, a decision that would have far-reaching consequences for the development and commercialization of telephone technology.

The simultaneous invention of the telephone raises intriguing questions about the nature of scientific discovery and innovation. It suggests that when the time is ripe for a particular invention - when the necessary precursor technologies are in place and the cultural and economic conditions are favorable - multiple inventors may arrive at similar solutions independently.

This phenomenon, known as multiple discovery or simultaneous invention, has occurred numerous times throughout history. Other famous examples include the independent formulation of calculus by Newton and Leibniz, and the simultaneous proposal of the theory of evolution by natural selection by Darwin and Wallace.

The Bell-Gray coincidence serves as a powerful reminder of the sometimes arbitrary nature of scientific credit and recognition. It highlights how small differences in timing or circumstance can have enormous historical consequences.

For Bell, the successful patent application led to fame, fortune, and a place in the pantheon of great inventors. For Gray, it led to relative obscurity, despite his significant contributions to electrical engineering and communication technology.

This story continues to fascinate historians of science and technology. It serves as a case study in the complex interplay between individual genius, societal needs, and the sometimes capricious nature of patent law and historical recognition.

The tale of Bell and Gray's simultaneous telephone inventions remains a compelling example of how great ideas can emerge in parallel, challenging our notions of individual genius and reminding us of the collaborative and cumulative nature of scientific and technological progress.

Chapter Fifty-Three

The Identical Strangers Meet: A Collision of Doppelgängers

In the realm of unlikely encounters, few stories are as striking as the tale of the identical strangers who quite literally collided with each other in 2002. This extraordinary event, which took place in Washington state, serves as a remarkable example of how reality can sometimes be stranger than fiction.

The incident occurred on a seemingly ordinary day in Spokane, Washington. Two men, both named James Alan Barnett and both 32 years old, were going about their daily routines. Neither had any idea that their lives were about to intersect in the most improbable of ways.

The first James Alan Barnett was driving his car through downtown Spokane when he was involved in a minor fender bender. As is customary in such situations, both drivers pulled over to exchange insurance information. It was at this moment that the truly extraordinary nature of the incident became apparent.

The driver of the other car was none other than the second James Alan Barnett. As the two men faced each other to exchange details, they were struck by an uncanny resemblance. Not only did they share the same name and age, but they also looked remarkably similar.

Stunned by this coincidence, the two James Alan Barnetts began to compare notes. They discovered that they were both born on the same day in 1970, although in different hospitals. Neither was adopted, and as far as they knew, they were not related in any way.

The similarities didn't end there. Both men worked in sales, though for different companies. They had similar builds, hair color, and even comparable styles of dress. The coincidence was so striking that bystanders who had gathered to check on the accident initially thought they were witnessing some kind of practical joke or hidden camera show.

News of this extraordinary encounter quickly spread, first locally and then nationally. The story captured the public imagination, sparking discussions about the nature of coincidence, the possibility of doppelgängers, and the potential for unknown family connections.

Geneticists and statisticians weighed in on the likelihood of such an occurrence. While they acknowledged that the chances of two unrelated individuals sharing so many similarities were extremely low, they also pointed out that in a world of billions of people, such coincidences, while rare, are not impossible.

For the two James Alan Barnetts, this chance encounter led to a friendship based on their shared experience of this extraordinary coincidence. They remained in touch, fascinated by the parallels in their lives and the unlikely circumstances that brought them together.

This story of the identical strangers serves as a powerful reminder of the unpredictable nature of life and the potential for extraordinary events to occur in the most mundane of circumstances. It challenges our understanding of probability and highlights the fascinating possibilities that can arise when chance alignments occur.

The tale of the two James Alan Barnetts continues to be recounted as one of the most remarkable examples of real-life coincidence, a story that blurs the line between reality and fiction and reminds us of the endless capacity for surprise in our everyday lives.

Chapter Fifty-Four

The Time-Traveling Obituary: A Premature Farewell

In the world of journalism, accuracy is paramount, especially when it comes to reporting on life and death. However, in 2012, a German magazine found itself at the center of a bizarre and somewhat comical error that seemed to defy the laws of time itself.

The incident involved the renowned American filmmaker George Hickenlooper, known for his documentaries and feature films. In 2012, a respected German film magazine decided to publish an obituary for Hickenlooper. There was just one problem: Hickenlooper had indeed passed away, but two years earlier, in 2010, at the age of 47.

The magazine had somehow published an obituary for a man who had died two years prior, but with the incorrect age of 95. This error created a surreal situation where it appeared as if Hickenlooper had lived for an additional 48 years after his actual death.

When the error was discovered, it caused quite a stir in both journalistic and film circles. Questions arose about how such a significant mistake could have been made by a reputable publication. Had the obituary been written years ago and accidentally published? Was it a case of mistaken identity? Or was it simply a series of unfortunate editorial errors?

The incident highlighted the challenges faced by media outlets in the digital age, where the pressure to publish quickly can sometimes lead to oversights. It also served as a reminder of the importance of fact-checking, especially when dealing with sensitive topics like death notices.

For Hickenlooper's family and friends, the error must have been a strange experience. To see a loved one's death announced years after the fact, and with such inaccurate information, likely brought up a mix of emotions - from confusion to perhaps a touch of dark humor.

The film community, too, found itself in an odd position. Many who knew Hickenlooper's work were aware of his untimely death in 2010. To see his passing announced again, as if he had lived to a ripe old age, created a sense of cognitive dissonance.

This incident of the time-traveling obituary serves as a fascinating example of how errors in reporting can sometimes create alternate realities, however briefly. It reminds us of the power of the written word and the responsibility that comes with it, especially when documenting the lives and deaths of public figures.

The story has since become a cautionary tale in journalism schools and newsrooms, used to illustrate the importance of thorough fact-checking and the potential consequences of publishing inaccurate information. It stands as a reminder that in the world of news, even the smallest details matter, and that sometimes, truth can indeed be stranger than fiction.

Chapter Fifty-Five

The Identical Twins' Accidents: A Tragic Symmetry

In the annals of tragic coincidences, few stories are as haunting and perplexing as the case of the Finnish identical twins who died in shockingly similar circumstances. This extraordinary event, which occurred in 2002, challenges our understanding of probability and raises questions about the mysterious connections that can exist between twins.

The protagonists of this tragic tale were two 70-year-old identical twin brothers living in Finland. Their story began on a seemingly ordinary Thursday when the first twin was riding his bicycle along a road in Raahe, a town on Finland's northwest coast. In a terrible accident, he was struck by a lorry and killed instantly.

News of this tragedy quickly spread through the family. However, the true shock was yet to come. Just two hours later and about 600 kilometers away, the second twin was also killed in a road accident. He too was riding a bicycle when he was hit by a truck in Helsinki.

The symmetry of these deaths is nothing short of astounding. Not only did both brothers die on the same day, but they also died in the same manner - cycling accidents involving large vehicles. The timeframe of just two hours between the incidents adds another layer of improbability to the event.

What makes this coincidence even more remarkable is that neither twin was aware of the other's accident. The second brother had no knowledge of his twin's fate when he set out on his own ill-fated bicycle ride.

News of this double tragedy quickly spread beyond Finland, capturing international attention. Many were fascinated by the seemingly impossible odds of such similar accidents befalling twins on the same day, especially given the distance between them.

The incident sparked discussions among scientists, particularly those studying twin behavior and genetics. Some speculated about the possibility of a shared predisposition to certain types of accidents, while others saw it as an extreme example of the mysterious connections often reported between twins.

For the family of the twins, the double loss was undoubtedly devastating. The simultaneous nature of the tragedies likely compounded their grief, while also perhaps providing a strange sort of solace in the symmetry of the brothers' fates.

This case of the identical twins' accidents serves as a poignant reminder of the unpredictable nature of life and death. It challenges our understanding of coincidence and probability, suggesting that there may be connections and patterns in the world that we do not yet fully comprehend.

The story continues to be cited in discussions about twin phenomena, the nature of coincidence, and the limits of statistical probability. It stands as a testament to the sometimes inexplicable symmetries that can occur in life, even in its final moments.

Chapter Fifty-Six

The Prophetic Painting: Salvador Dalí's Surreal Foresight

In the realm of art and prophecy, few stories are as intriguing as that of Salvador Dalí's seemingly prescient painting created on the eve of the Spanish Civil War. This extraordinary coincidence, which blurs the line between artistic intuition and premonition, has fascinated art historians and coincidence enthusiasts for decades.

The story centers around a painting Dalí created in 1936 titled "Soft Construction with Boiled Beans (Premonition of Civil War)". What makes this work remarkable is not just its striking surrealist imagery, but the timing of its creation and the events that followed.

Dalí began work on this painting in 1936, months before the outbreak of the Spanish Civil War. The artwork depicts a large, distorted human figure tearing itself apart, set against a barren landscape. The figure is grotesque and tortured, seeming to embody the violence and self-destruction of war.

The most astonishing aspect of this painting is that Dalí completed it just months before the Spanish Civil War actually began in July 1936. The artist himself claimed that he had a premonition of the coming conflict, which he channeled into this disturbing and prophetic work.

When the war did break out, the painting took on a new significance. Many saw it as evidence of Dalí's uncanny ability to sense the tensions brewing in Spanish society and translate them into visual form. The torn figure became a powerful symbol of a nation tearing itself apart through civil conflict.

Art historians have long debated the true nature of Dalí's "premonition". Some argue that as an politically aware artist, Dalí was simply attuned to the escalating tensions in Spain and expressed them through his art. Others see it as a more mysterious case of artistic foresight, perhaps tapping into the collective unconscious of a nation on the brink of war.

Regardless of the explanation, the timing and content of "Soft Construction with Boiled Beans" remain remarkable. The painting has since become one of Dalí's most famous works, not just for its artistic merit, but for its eerie connection to historical events.

This incident highlights the complex relationship between art and society, showing how artists can sometimes act as a barometer for social and political tensions. It also raises intriguing questions about the nature of creativity and intuition, and the potential for art to tap into deeper currents of human experience and foreshadow future events.

The story of Dalí's prophetic painting continues to captivate those interested in art, history, and the mysterious workings of human creativity. It stands as a powerful example of how art can sometimes seem to transcend its immediate context, reaching into the future in ways that challenge our understanding of time and perception.

Chapter Fifty-Seven

The Prophetic Novel: Morgan Robertson's Titanic Premonition

In the annals of literary prophecy, few stories are as chilling and precise as Morgan Robertson's novella "Futility, or the Wreck of the Titan." Published in 1898, a full 14 years before the tragic sinking of the RMS Titanic, Robertson's tale bore such striking similarities to the real-life disaster that it has since been hailed as one of the most remarkable premonitions in literary history.

Robertson's novella tells the story of a supposedly unsinkable ocean liner named Titan. This fictional ship, like its real-life counterpart, was one of the largest vessels of its time. The Titan, described as the largest craft afloat and the greatest of the works of men, bore an uncanny resemblance to the Titanic in both its features and its fate.

The similarities between fiction and reality are nothing short of astonishing:

1. Both ships were described as "unsinkable."

2. The Titan and the Titanic were similar in size, with the Titan being 800 feet long and the Titanic 882.5 feet.

3. Both ships had three propellers and two masts.

4. Both vessels could carry about 3,000 people.

5. Both had too few lifeboats for the number of people on board.

6. Both struck an iceberg in the North Atlantic in April, around midnight.

7. Both sank, resulting in massive loss of life.

The eerie parallels extend even further. In Robertson's story, the Titan was traveling at 25 knots when it struck the iceberg, while the Titanic was moving at 22.5 knots. Both ships sank about 400 miles from Newfoundland, and both events resulted in the deaths of more than half of their passengers and crew.

When the Titanic sank in 1912, the similarities to Robertson's novel were quickly noticed, leading to accusations of clairvoyance or some form of precognition. Robertson himself claimed that the similarities were a result of his extensive knowledge of shipbuilding and maritime trends, rather than any psychic abilities.

This incident has since become a favorite topic among those interested in prophecies, premonitions, and the sometimes uncanny ability of fiction to predict future events. It has been the subject of numerous books, articles, and documentaries, each attempting to explain the extraordinary coincidence.

Some see it as evidence of the power of human intuition and imagination, while others view it as a remarkable but ultimately explainable coincidence. Skeptics point out that given the number of novels written and the inevitability of maritime disasters, some overlap between fiction and reality is bound to occur.

Regardless of how one interprets it, the story of "Futility" remains one of the most famous examples of apparent precognition in literature. It serves as a haunting reminder of the thin line between fiction and reality, and the mysterious ways in which art can sometimes seem to predict life.

Chapter Fifty-Eight

The Prophetic Chess Game: Kasparov's Uncanny Foreshadowing

In the world of chess, where human intellect has long reigned supreme, few stories are as intriguing as the tale of Garry Kasparov's prophetic chess game. This remarkable incident, which occurred in 1985, seemed to foreshadow a pivotal moment in the history of artificial intelligence and chess that would unfold over a decade later.

The story begins in Hamburg, Germany, where Garry Kasparov, then a rising star in the chess world, participated in a simultaneous exhibition match against 32 chess computers. Such exhibitions, where a single player competes against multiple opponents simultaneously, were common ways for top players to showcase their skills.

Kasparov, known for his aggressive and dominant playing style, handily defeated 31 of the 32 computer opponents. However, one game stood out - his match against a program called "Microchess." Unlike its defeated digital brethren, Microchess managed to secure a draw against the future world champion.

At the time, this result was seen as a curiosity rather than a portent. Computers were still far from being able to consistently challenge top human players, and Kasparov would go on to become the world chess champion later that same year.

The true significance of this game would only become apparent 12 years later, in 1997. In a highly publicized match, Kasparov faced off against IBM's Deep Blue, a supercomputer specifically designed for chess. In a shocking turn of events, Deep Blue defeated Kasparov, becoming the first computer to beat a reigning world champion in a match under standard chess tournament time controls.

The parallels between the 1985 exhibition and the 1997 match are striking. In both cases, Kasparov found himself unable to secure victory against a computer opponent, with the earlier draw against Microchess seemingly foreshadowing his later defeat by Deep Blue.

This coincidence has fascinated chess enthusiasts and technology historians alike. Some see it as an early indicator of the potential of artificial intelligence, a small hint of the computational power that would eventually challenge human supremacy in chess. Others view it as a quirk of fate, a random alignment that only gained significance in hindsight.

For Kasparov himself, the 1985 exhibition likely held little significance at the time. Yet, after his defeat by Deep Blue, one wonders if he ever reflected on that drawn game against Microchess, seeing in it a subtle warning of the challenge that lay ahead.

The story of Kasparov's prophetic chess game serves as a fascinating example of how seemingly minor events can sometimes foreshadow major shifts in human history. It highlights the rapid advancement of computer technology and artificial intelligence, fields that have progressed from being curiosities to serious competitors to human intellect in specific domains.

This tale continues to be recounted in discussions about the history of chess and the development of AI. It stands as a reminder of the sometimes surprising ways in which the past can hint at the future, and how even in the most rigorous and logical of pursuits, there's always room for a touch of uncanny coincidence.

Chapter Fifty-Nine

The Simultaneous Discoveries: Newton and Leibniz's Calculus

In the annals of scientific history, few coincidences are as significant as the simultaneous development of calculus by Isaac Newton and Gottfried Wilhelm Leibniz. This extraordinary parallel discovery, which occurred in the late 17th century, not only revolutionized mathematics but also sparked one of the most famous priority disputes in the history of science.

Isaac Newton, the English physicist and mathematician, began developing his ideas on calculus as early as 1665. However, he didn't publish his work immediately, keeping much of it private. Meanwhile, across the English Channel, Gottfried Leibniz, a German polymath, independently started working on similar mathematical concepts in the 1670s.

The crux of their discoveries lay in the development of a mathematical system that could describe and quantify change - the fundamental principle of calculus. Both men approached the problem from slightly different angles, with Newton focusing on what he called "fluxions" and Leibniz developing a more elegant notational system that is still widely used today.

What makes this coincidence truly remarkable is not just that they developed similar ideas, but that they did so without any significant communication or knowledge of each other's work. The intellectual climate of Europe at the time, with its rapid advancements in physics and mathematics, had created a perfect storm for this kind of breakthrough.

When Leibniz published his work on calculus in 1684, it sparked a controversy. Newton's supporters accused Leibniz of plagiarism, insisting that he must have had access to Newton's unpublished work. This led to a bitter dispute that lasted for years and divided the mathematical community.

Modern historians generally agree that both men developed calculus independently, attributing the simultaneous discovery to the intellectual zeitgeist of the era. This incident serves as a prime example of multiple discovery in science - the phenomenon where similar discoveries are made by scientists working independently of each other.

The simultaneous discovery of calculus by Newton and Leibniz highlights how scientific progress often occurs when the time is ripe, with multiple minds converging on similar ideas. It reminds us that even the most groundbreaking discoveries can emerge in parallel, shaped by the collective knowledge and questions of an era.

This coincidence not only gave us two different approaches to calculus but also spurred further developments in mathematics as supporters of each mathematician worked to refine and expand their theories. Today, elements of both Newton's and Leibniz's work are recognized in modern calculus, a testament to their shared, yet independent, genius.

Chapter Sixty

The Unlucky Passenger: A Tale of Near Misses

In the realm of coincidences, few stories are as chilling and thought-provoking as that of the unlucky passenger who twice narrowly escaped death by missing the same ill-fated flight, one year apart. This extraordinary tale of near misses serves as a stark reminder of the thin line between fate and chance.

The story begins in 1950 when a man, whose name has been lost to history, was scheduled to board a flight from a major airport. Due to an unexpected delay in his journey to the airport, he missed his flight by mere minutes. Frustrated and inconvenienced, he had no idea that this delay had just saved his life. Shortly after takeoff, the plane he was meant to be on experienced catastrophic mechanical failure and crashed, resulting in the loss of all lives on board.

Shaken by his narrow escape, the man likely spent the following year reflecting on his fortune. However, fate wasn't done with him yet. In a twist that seems almost too incredible to be true, the same scenario played out again exactly one year later.

In 1951, the man once again found himself rushing to catch the very same flight on the same airline, following the same route. And once again, due to an unexpected delay, he missed the flight. In an eerie echo of the previous year's events, this plane also crashed shortly after takeoff, once again with no survivors.

The odds of missing the same flight twice due to delays, with both flights ending in crashes, are astronomically low. This double near-miss quickly became a topic of fascination for those interested in coincidences and the nature of fate.

For the man at the center of this story, these events must have been profoundly impactful. To twice escape death by such narrow margins, and in such similar circumstances, would likely have led to deep reflection on the nature of luck, fate, and mortality.

This incident raises intriguing questions about the role of chance in our lives. Was it mere coincidence, or was there some greater force at work? The story has been cited by some as evidence of destiny or divine intervention, while others see it as an extreme example of random chance.

Chapter Sixty-One

The Prophetic Poem: Katharine Lee Bates' Visionary Verse

In the realm of literary premonitions, few examples are as striking as the case of Katharine Lee Bates and her seemingly prophetic poem about airships. This remarkable incident, which occurred at the turn of the 20th century, showcases the sometimes uncanny ability of artists to envision future technologies.

Katharine Lee Bates, an American poet and professor best known for writing the lyrics to "America the Beautiful," penned a lesser-known but equally intriguing poem in 1898. The poem, titled "The Great Airship," described a massive flying vessel in the sky, a concept that was still firmly in the realm of science fiction at the time.

What makes this poem truly remarkable is that it preceded the first successful flight of a rigid airship, or Zeppelin, by nearly 14 years. Count Ferdinand von Zeppelin wouldn't launch his first successful airship until 1900, and it wasn't until 1912 that Zeppelins began commercial passenger flights.

Bates' poem described the airship in vivid detail:

"Lo, in the twilight gloom,The great airship doth loom,Dim as a pallid ghost,Leading a shadowy host."

The accuracy of her description is uncanny. She envisioned a large, spectral presence in the sky, much like how early Zeppelins would have appeared to observers on the ground. The poem goes on to describe the airship's movement and its impact on those witnessing it, capturing the awe and wonder that early airships indeed inspired.

This poetic premonition raises intriguing questions about the nature of creativity and foresight. Was Bates simply extrapolating from the scientific discussions and speculative fiction of her time, or did she possess some sort of intuitive glimpse into the future?

It's worth noting that the concept of airships wasn't entirely new in 1898. Balloons had been used for aerial observation since the late 18th century, and various designs for dirigible airships had been proposed. However, Bates' specific vision of a "great airship" that could carry passengers was remarkably prescient.

This incident serves as a fascinating example of how artists and writers can sometimes anticipate future developments with surprising accuracy. It highlights the power of imagination and the ways in which creative minds can envision possibilities beyond the current limits of technology.

The story of Katharine Lee Bates' prophetic poem continues to intrigue literary scholars and aviation enthusiasts alike. It stands as a testament to the sometimes mysterious connection between artistic vision and technological progress, reminding us that today's flights of fancy may well be tomorrow's reality.

Chapter Sixty-Two

The Reincarnated Golfer: A Young Prodigy's Past-Life Memories

In the rolling hills of Scotland, a country renowned for its golf courses and rich sporting history, an extraordinary tale unfolded that challenges our understanding of talent, memory, and the possibility of past lives. This is the story of a young boy who demonstrated an inexplicable talent for golf and claimed to possess memories of a professional golfer's life from the 1930s.

The protagonist of this remarkable story is a boy who, from the moment he could walk, showed an uncanny affinity for golf. At an age when most children are still learning to tie their shoelaces, this young prodigy was demonstrating golf swings that professional players spend years perfecting. His ability to read greens, select clubs, and execute complex shots left observers astounded.

What made this case truly extraordinary, however, were the boy's claims about the source of his talent. From a very young age, he began to speak about memories of a life as a professional golfer in the 1930s. He described in vivid detail the courses he had played, the tournaments he had won, and even the fellow golfers he had competed against - all events that had occurred decades before his birth.

The boy's parents, initially skeptical, were amazed by the accuracy and specificity of his recollections. He mentioned obscure rules that were only in effect during the '30s, described the exact layouts of historic courses that had since been redesigned, and even recalled the scores of matches played long ago.

Golf historians and researchers, intrigued by the boy's claims, began to investigate. They were astounded to find that many of the details he provided matched historical records perfectly. The boy was able to describe events and people from the 1930s golfing world with an accuracy that seemed impossible for someone of his age to have researched or learned through conventional means.

This case quickly caught the attention of those interested in the concept of reincarnation. Some saw it as compelling evidence for the existence of past lives, while skeptics searched for alternative explanations, such as cryptomnesia - the emergence of memories acquired in ways the individual cannot recall.

For the golfing community, the boy's incredible talent was undeniable, regardless of its source. He quickly became a sensation in junior golf tournaments, with many predicting a future career as a top professional player.

This extraordinary tale of the reincarnated golfer serves as a fascinating intersection of sports, psychology, and the paranormal. It challenges our understanding of how skills are acquired and raises profound questions about the nature of consciousness and memory.

Whether viewed as evidence of reincarnation, an unexplained case of genetic memory, or simply an extraordinary coincidence, the story of the young golf prodigy with memories of a past life continues to captivate and perplex those who hear it. It stands as a reminder of the mysteries that still surround human consciousness and the sometimes inexplicable nature of talent and memory.

Chapter Sixty-Three

The Matching DNA: An Impossible Genetic Coincidence

In the vast realm of genetic diversity, where the odds of two unrelated individuals sharing identical DNA are astronomically low, a case emerged that defied scientific explanation and challenged our understanding of genetic uniqueness. This is the extraordinary story of two men who discovered they had nearly identical DNA sequences, a coincidence so rare it was estimated to have a probability of one in a trillion.

The tale begins with two men, let's call them John and Michael, who lived in different parts of the United States and had no known familial connection. Both had independently decided to undergo genetic testing, a increasingly common practice in the age of personalized medicine and ancestry exploration.

When the results came back, the laboratory technicians were baffled. The genetic profiles of John and Michael were so similar that the initial assumption was a sample mix-up had occurred. However, after careful rechecking and retesting, it became clear that this was no mistake - the two men indeed shared an unprecedented level of genetic similarity.

In typical cases, even close relatives like siblings share only about 50% of their DNA. Identical twins are the exception, sharing nearly 100% of their genetic material. John and Michael, however, showed a match rate of over 99.9%, despite having no known relation and being born to different parents in different parts of the country.

The discovery sent shockwaves through the genetic research community. Scientists from various institutions began studying this extraordinary case, seeking to understand how such a genetic coincidence could occur. Theories ranged from an unknown type of genetic copying mechanism to the possibility of a long-forgotten family connection.

For John and Michael, the revelation was life-changing. Two strangers suddenly found themselves linked in a way that defied explanation. They met and discovered that despite their genetic similarity, they had led very different lives with distinct personalities, interests, and physical characteristics - a finding that further intrigued researchers studying the influence of environment on genetic expression.

This case raised profound questions about genetic diversity and identity. If two unrelated individuals could share such similar DNA, what did it mean for our understanding of genetic uniqueness? How many other such cases might exist undetected? The implications for fields ranging from forensic science to genetic medicine were enormous.

The story of John and Michael's matching DNA became a topic of fascination not just in scientific circles but in the public imagination as well. It challenged our notions of individuality and the role of genetics in shaping who we are.

As research continues, this extraordinary genetic coincidence remains a mystery. It stands as a humbling reminder of how much we still have to learn about the complex interplay of genes and the occasional tricks that nature can play. The case of the matching DNA continues to inspire scientific inquiry and philosophical debate, embodying the wonder and unpredictability of human genetics.

Chapter Sixty-Four

The Immortal Jellyfish: Nature's Age-Defying Wonder

In the vast and mysterious depths of the ocean, a discovery was made in 1988 that challenged our fundamental understanding of life and death. This is the story of Turritopsis dohrnii, commonly known as the "immortal jellyfish," a creature that seems to defy one of nature's most unbreakable rules: the inevitability of death.

The discovery of this extraordinary species occurred off the coast of Italy. Marine biologists were studying various jellyfish species when they encountered a tiny, bell-shaped creature barely 4.5 millimeters across. Initially, it seemed unremarkable, just another of the countless jellyfish species that populate the world's oceans.

However, as researchers continued to observe this species, they noticed something extraordinary. When faced with environmental stress or physical damage, instead of dying, the Turritopsis dohrnii would transform itself back into its juvenile polyp stage. This process, known as transdifferentiation, essentially allows the jellyfish to reverse its life cycle.

In essence, when threatened with death, the immortal jellyfish can revert to its earliest stage of life and begin the cycle anew. It's as if a butterfly, instead of dying, could transform back into a caterpillar and start its life over again. This ability theoretically allows the Turritopsis dohrnii to live indefinitely, barring disease or predation.

The implications of this discovery were staggering. Here was a complex, multicellular organism that appeared to have achieved biological immortality. Scientists around the world were captivated by the potential insights this creature could offer into the aging process and the nature of death itself.

Research into the immortal jellyfish has since become a significant field of study. Scientists are working to understand the cellular mechanisms that allow for this remarkable transformation. The hope is that insights gained from studying the Turritopsis dohrnii might one day lead to breakthroughs in human medicine, potentially offering new approaches to treating age-related diseases or even extending human lifespan.

The discovery of the immortal jellyfish also raises profound philosophical questions. In a world where death has always been seen as the great equalizer, what does it mean for a creature to potentially live forever? How does this challenge our understanding of the life cycle and the role of death in nature?

From an evolutionary perspective, the immortal jellyfish presents a fascinating case study. While the ability to indefinitely renew oneself might seem like an overwhelming advantage, it hasn't led to the species dominating the oceans. This suggests that immortality, at least in nature, may not be as advantageous as it first appears.

The story of the immortal jellyfish serves as a powerful reminder of the wonders still waiting to be discovered in the natural world. It challenges our preconceptions about the fundamentals of life and death, and opens up new avenues for scientific exploration. As research continues, the tiny Turritopsis dohrnii continues to captivate scientists and the public alike, embodying the endless possibilities and mysteries of the natural world.

Chapter Sixty-Five

The Predicting Parrot: A Feathered Forecaster

In the bustling metropolis of New York City, where the unexpected is often the norm, a peculiar incident occurred that left residents and seismologists alike scratching their heads. This is the tale of a pet parrot whose seemingly nonsensical squawks took on an eerie significance in the days leading up to a minor earthquake.

The story centers around a African Grey parrot named Charlie, known for its intelligence and ability to mimic human speech. Charlie lived with its owner, Sarah, in a small apartment in Manhattan. While the bird had a extensive vocabulary, it had never before uttered the word "earthquake."

However, about a week before the incident, Charlie began repeatedly squawking "earthquake" with increasing frequency. At first, Sarah found it amusing, wondering where her feathered friend had picked up the new word. As the days passed and Charlie's insistence grew, Sarah's amusement turned to concern.

She mentioned Charlie's odd behavior to friends and family, some of whom jokingly suggested she should prepare for a seismic event. Little did they know how prophetic those jokes would turn out to be.

On the morning of the tremor, Charlie's squawks reached a fever pitch. The parrot seemed agitated, repeating "earthquake" almost non-stop. A few hours later, a minor earthquake, measuring 2.6 on the Richter scale, shook the city. While it caused no damage, it was significant enough to be felt by many residents and reported in the local news.

The coincidence between Charlie's behavior and the seismic event quickly became a topic of fascination. Local media picked up the story, and Sarah found herself and Charlie at the center of an unexpected media frenzy.

Experts were consulted to explain the phenomenon. Some suggested that animals, including birds, might be sensitive to subtle changes in the environment that precede earthquakes, such as shifts in the Earth's magnetic field or releases of gases from the ground.

Skeptics, however, pointed out that parrots often repeat words randomly, and the timing could be pure coincidence. They argued that confirmation bias might be at play, with people remembering the correct prediction while forgetting any incorrect ones.

Regardless of the explanation, the story of the predicting parrot captured the public's imagination. It sparked discussions about animal cognition, the potential for earthquake prediction, and the mysterious ways in which nature might communicate impending dangers.

For Sarah and Charlie, life eventually returned to normal, but their brush with notoriety left them with an extraordinary tale to tell. The incident serves as a reminder of the often surprising connections between humans, animals, and the natural world, and the potential for remarkable coincidences in the most unexpected of places.

Chapter Sixty-Six

The Time Slip: A Hotel Lost in Time

In the summer of 1979, two couples from England embarked on what they thought would be a routine vacation in Spain. Little did they know that their journey would take them not just across geographical boundaries, but seemingly through time itself, in one of the most puzzling cases of a supposed "time slip" ever recorded.

The couples, let's call them the Smiths and the Johnsons, were driving through the Spanish countryside when they decided to stop for the night. They came across a quaint, old-fashioned hotel that seemed charmingly out of place in the modern landscape. Attracted by its vintage appeal, they decided to stay the night.

Upon checking in, the couples noticed several odd details. The hotel staff wore outdated uniforms, and the decor seemed to belong to a much earlier era. The room rates were surprisingly low, quoted in old Spanish currency. Despite these peculiarities, they enjoyed a comfortable night's stay and continued their journey the next morning.

It was only when they tried to find the hotel again on their return trip that the true strangeness of their experience became apparent. The hotel was nowhere to be found. Perplexed, they asked locals about the establishment, only to be told that no such hotel existed in the area.

Upon returning to England, the couples' curiosity led them to conduct further research. To their astonishment, they found old photographs of a hotel that matched their description perfectly. However, historical records showed that this hotel had been demolished decades ago, long before their visit in 1979.

The story quickly caught the attention of paranormal researchers and time slip enthusiasts. Many theories were proposed to explain the couples' experience. Some suggested they had somehow slipped through a crack in time, briefly visiting the Spain of the past. Others proposed the idea of residual haunting, where a place or event leaves an imprint on time that can occasionally be experienced by sensitive individuals.

Skeptics, naturally, had their own explanations. They suggested the couples might have misremembered details, conflating their experience with old photographs they might have seen. Others proposed the possibility of an elaborate hoax or a shared delusion.

Regardless of the explanation, the story of the vanishing hotel has become a classic in the annals of time slip phenomena. It raises intriguing questions about the nature of time and reality, and the potential for past, present, and future to intersect in ways we don't yet understand.

For the Smiths and Johnsons, their Spanish vacation became an unexpected journey into the unknown, leaving them with a tale that continues to baffle and fascinate decades later. Their experience serves as a reminder of the mysteries that still exist in our world, and the potential for extraordinary encounters in the most ordinary of circumstances.

Chapter Sixty-Seven

The Simultaneous Suicides: A Tragic Coincidence

In 2007, a small town in Belgium became the unlikely setting for one of the most extraordinary and tragic coincidences in recent memory. This somber tale involves two strangers whose paths crossed in the most unexpected and heartbreaking of ways, challenging our understanding of chance and the interconnectedness of human lives.

On a quiet autumn evening, two individuals—a man and a woman, both in their early forties—independently made their way to an isolated spot on the outskirts of town. This location, a nondescript clearing in a small wooded area, was not known as a popular destination. It was simply a quiet, out-of-the-way place that happened to catch the attention of both individuals.

What makes this incident so remarkable is that these two people, who had never met and had no connection to each other, had both chosen this specific location to end their lives. They arrived within minutes of each other, each unaware of the other's presence or intentions.

The tragic scene was discovered the next morning by a local hiker. The authorities were baffled by the circumstances. Initial investigations ruled out any form of foul play or suicide pact. It became clear that this was a case of two separate suicides that had, by some twist of fate, occurred at the same time and place.

As the story unfolded, it captured national attention. People were struck by the improbability of such an occurrence. The odds of two strangers independently choosing the same obscure location to end their lives, and arriving there at almost the same moment, seemed astronomical.

The incident sparked discussions about mental health awareness and the importance of suicide prevention. Many wondered if the tragedy could have been prevented if either individual had encountered another person during their final moments.

Psychologists and sociologists studied the case, exploring the possible factors that might have led both individuals to choose that particular spot. Some suggested that certain locations might have characteristics that appeal to people in a suicidal state of mind, though this theory remains speculative.

For the families of the deceased, the coincidence added an extra layer of complexity to their grief. While grappling with their loss, they also had to contend with the public attention the unusual circumstances had attracted.

This tragic event serves as a somber reminder of the unpredictable nature of human behavior and the sometimes inexplicable ways in which our lives can intersect. It highlights the silent struggles many people face and the importance of reaching out to those in need.

The simultaneous suicides in Belgium remain a poignant example of how coincidence can manifest in even the most tragic of circumstances, leaving us to ponder the mysterious threads that connect human experiences and the profound impact of chance encounters—or in this case, near-encounters—on our lives.

Chapter Sixty-Eight

The Prophetic Painting: An Artist's Unconscious Vision

In 1967, an amateur artist named Robert Jenkins sat down at his easel in his small apartment in Manchester, England. With no particular scene in mind, he began to paint, letting his brush strokes flow freely across the canvas. What emerged was a serene landscape featuring a quaint cottage nestled among rolling hills, with a distinctive gnarled oak tree standing prominently in the foreground.

At the time, Jenkins thought little of the painting. It was pleasing to the eye, but he considered it nothing more than a product of his imagination. He hung it in his living room, where it remained for the next three decades, a quiet backdrop to his daily life.

Fast forward to 1997. Jenkins, now retired, decided to fulfill a lifelong dream of traveling the world. His journey took him to New Zealand, a country he had never visited before. One day, while exploring the countryside of the South Island, Jenkins rounded a bend in the road and was struck by an overwhelming sense of déjà vu.

Before him lay a scene that was eerily familiar: a cottage among rolling hills, with a gnarled oak tree in the foreground. It was, in almost every detail, the exact landscape he had painted 30 years earlier, thousands of miles away in Manchester.

Stunned by the similarity, Jenkins took photographs and, upon returning home, compared them to his painting. The resemblance was uncanny. The shape of the hills, the position of the cottage, and most strikingly, the unique form of the oak tree, all matched his decades-old artwork with remarkable precision.

News of this extraordinary coincidence quickly spread. Art experts examined the original painting and confirmed its age, ruling out the possibility that Jenkins had painted it after his trip. Psychologists and parapsychologists became interested in the case, seeing it as a potential example of precognition or clairvoyance.

Various theories were proposed to explain the phenomenon. Some suggested that Jenkins might have seen a photograph or film of the New Zealand landscape years earlier and subconsciously incorporated it into his painting. Others proposed more esoteric explanations, such as the concept of morphic resonance or the idea of a collective unconscious containing information about distant places and future events.

For Jenkins, the experience was profound and life-changing. He began to question the nature of creativity and inspiration, wondering about the source of the images that artists produce. The incident sparked a renewed passion for painting in him, as he explored the boundaries between imagination and reality in his art.

This case of the prophetic painting serves as a fascinating example of the mysteries that still surround human creativity and perception. It challenges our understanding of the relationship between art and reality, and raises intriguing questions about the potential for unconscious knowledge or foresight.

Whether viewed as an extraordinary coincidence or something more mysterious, the story of Robert Jenkins and his inadvertently prophetic landscape continues to captivate those who hear it, reminding us of the often inexplicable connections between imagination and the physical world.

Chapter Sixty-Nine

The Genetic Neighbors: A DNA Reunion Next Door

In a small town in Oregon, a story unfolded that seemed more fitting for a heartwarming Hollywood script than real life. This tale of coincidence and connection centers around two neighbors, Sarah Thompson and Mike Anderson, who lived next door to each other for over a decade without realizing they shared a profound biological bond.

Sarah and Mike had been friendly neighbors since Sarah moved in 12 years ago. They'd exchange pleasantries over the fence, attend the same community events, and even water each other's plants during vacations. Their relationship was cordial but casual, with neither having any inkling of a deeper connection.

The revelation began when both Sarah and Mike, independently of each other, decided to use popular DNA testing services to explore their family histories. Sarah, an adopted child, was curious about her biological roots. Mike, having recently become a father himself, wanted to learn more about his family's medical history.

When the results came back, both Sarah and Mike were in for the shock of their lives. The DNA tests revealed that they were, in fact, biological siblings. The system had matched their DNA profiles, indicating a high probability of a first-degree relation.

Stunned by this discovery, Sarah and Mike arranged to meet and discuss the results. As they compared notes, the truth emerged: they were indeed brother and sister, separated in childhood when Sarah was put up for adoption. Mike, being slightly older, had vague memories of a baby sister but had been told she died in infancy.

The coincidence of them ending up as neighbors in the same small town, out of all the places they could have lived, was astounding. They had lived side by side for years, unknowingly passing their sibling every day.

As news of their discovery spread, it captured the imagination of their community and soon, the national media. Their story became a sensation, with many marveling at the incredible odds of such a reunion occurring.

For Sarah and Mike, the revelation transformed their relationship overnight. They went from being casual neighbors to family, working to build a sibling bond that had been denied to them for decades. They delved into their shared history, piecing together the circumstances that led to their separation and marveling at the twist of fate that brought them back together.

Their story sparked discussions about the power of DNA testing to uncover hidden family connections and the potential for such technologies to reshape our understanding of family and identity. It also raised questions about the nature of kinship and whether blood ties inevitably create a bond, even when discovered later in life.

The tale of the genetic neighbors serves as a powerful reminder of the unexpected ways our lives can intersect with others, and the profound impact that chance and circumstance can have on our personal narratives. It stands as a testament to the sometimes miraculous nature of coincidence and the enduring power of family connections, even when hidden for years.

Chapter Seventy

The Recurring Numbers: A Lottery Winner's Numerical Omen

In the realm of coincidences, few stories are as captivating as that of Sarah Miller, a woman whose encounter with recurring numbers led to an extraordinary twist of fate. This tale of numerical synchronicity culminated in a lottery win that defied all odds and left many questioning the nature of chance and premonition.

Sarah's story began in early November when she started noticing the numbers 1123 appearing with unusual frequency in her daily life. At first, it was subtle - a receipt total, a license plate, or a phone number. But as the days passed, the appearances became more frequent and increasingly difficult to ignore.

She saw 1123 on digital clocks, page numbers, and even in seemingly random places like the number of likes on a social media post. Friends and family initially dismissed her observations as selective attention, a phenomenon where one notices something more once they start looking for it.

However, the frequency and specificity of the number's appearances began to unnerve Sarah. She started documenting each occurrence, filling a notebook with dates, times, and locations of each 1123 sighting. As the list grew, so did her conviction that these numbers held some significance.

The crescendo of this numerical phenomenon occurred on November 23rd - 11/23 in the American date format. On this day, on a whim and with a sense of fateful inevitability, Sarah decided to play the lottery using the numbers that had been haunting her for weeks.

In a turn of events that seems almost too scripted to be real, Sarah's numbers came up. She had won a substantial jackpot, turning her weeks of numerical obsession into a life-changing windfall.

News of Sarah's win, coupled with the story of the recurring numbers, quickly spread. It captured the public imagination, sparking discussions about numerology, synchronicity, and the nature of luck. Some saw it as proof of a hidden order in the universe, while skeptics argued it was merely an extreme case of coincidence amplified by confirmation bias.

Psychologists and statisticians weighed in, debating the likelihood of such an occurrence and exploring the human tendency to find patterns in randomness. For many, Sarah's story reinforced the allure of finding meaning in numbers and the eternal hope of predicting the unpredictable.

For Sarah herself, the experience was transformative. Beyond the financial windfall, it left her with a profound sense of connection to the hidden workings of the world. She became an object of fascination, with many seeking her out for luck or insight into the numerical mysteries of the universe.

This extraordinary tale of recurring numbers and lottery luck serves as a reminder of the mysterious ways in which patterns can emerge in our lives. It challenges our understanding of coincidence and probability, leaving us to wonder about the fine line between random chance and meaningful synchronicity in our daily experiences.

Chapter Seventy-One

The Switched-at-Birth Reunion: A 50-Year Mystery Solved

In the annals of unlikely reunions, few stories are as extraordinary as that of Linda Johnson and Mary Williams. Their tale, which unfolded at a college reunion half a century after their births, is a testament to the sometimes unbelievable twists of fate that can shape our lives.

The story begins in a small hospital in the Midwest in 1950. Two babies were born on the same day: one to the Johnson family and one to the Williams family. In a mix-up that would go undetected for decades, the infants were accidentally switched before being sent home with their respective families.

Linda grew up as a Johnson, and Mary as a Williams. Both led normal lives, unaware of the mistake that had occurred on the day of their births. They attended the same college in the late 1960s but, despite being in the same year, never crossed paths during their time there.

Fast forward to 2000, when their alma mater hosted a 50-year reunion for the class of 1970. Linda and Mary, now both 50 years old, attended the event, each looking forward to reconnecting with old classmates. It was here, in a twist of fate that seems almost too coincidental to be true, that they met for the first time.

The initial connection was sparked by an offhand comment about birth dates. As they chatted, they discovered they shared not only a birthday but were born in the same hospital. Intrigued by the coincidence, they began to share more details about their lives.

As the conversation deepened, discrepancies began to emerge. Family traits, genetic predispositions, and even blood types didn't seem to align with what they knew of their families. A seed of doubt was planted, leading both women to investigate further.

DNA tests confirmed what they had begun to suspect: They had been switched at birth. The revelation was shocking, upending five decades of family history and personal identity for both women.

The news of their discovery spread quickly, captivating the public with its blend of incredulity and poignancy. It raised questions about the nature of family, nurture versus nature, and the role of chance in shaping our lives.

For Linda and Mary, the revelation led to a complex emotional journey. They had to grapple with the shock of the discovery, the joy of finding a biological connection, and the challenge of integrating this new reality into their existing family relationships.

Their story also sparked discussions about hospital protocols and the importance of fail-safe systems in newborn care. It served as a reminder of how a single mistake can have profound, lifelong consequences.

The tale of Linda and Mary's switched-at-birth reunion stands as an extraordinary example of how truth can be stranger than fiction. It reminds us of the incredible coincidences that can occur in life and the potential for unexpected discoveries to reshape our understanding of who we are and where we come from.

Chapter Seventy-Two

The Prophetic Dream Job: A Visionary Career Path

In the realm of dreams and premonitions, few stories are as striking as that of Michael Chen, a man whose nocturnal vision led him to an uncanny encounter with his future workplace. This tale of prophetic dreaming challenges our understanding of coincidence and raises intriguing questions about the nature of foresight and destiny.

Michael's story began on a nondescript night in 2010. In his dream, he found himself working in a distinctive office space. The dream was vivid and detailed, featuring a unique layout with an open-plan design, vibrant blue walls, and a striking piece of modern art hanging in the reception area. Michael, not one to typically remember his dreams, was so struck by the clarity of this vision that he sketched the office layout and made notes about its distinctive features upon waking.

At the time, Michael was employed in a completely different field and had no immediate plans to change careers. He filed away his sketch and notes, attributing the dream to an overactive imagination or perhaps a subconscious desire for a new work environment.

Five years passed, and Michael's career took an unexpected turn. After being laid off from his long-time job, he began searching for new opportunities. One day, he came across a job listing that intrigued him, despite it being in an industry he had never considered before. He applied, was called for an interview, and arrived at the company's office building with a sense of nervous anticipation.

As the elevator doors opened onto the office floor, Michael was struck by an overwhelming sense of déjà vu. The layout before him was eerily familiar – an open-plan design, vibrant blue walls, and there, hanging in the reception area, was the exact piece of modern art he had seen in his dream years ago.

Stunned by the similarity, Michael retrieved the sketch he had made of his dream office. The resemblance was uncanny, down to the smallest details. It was as if he had drawn a blueprint of this very office five years before he had ever set foot in it.

The interviewers were impressed by Michael's qualifications, but were astounded when he shared his story and produced the old sketch. This extraordinary coincidence seemed to seal the deal, and Michael was offered the job on the spot.

News of Michael's prophetic dream quickly spread throughout the company and eventually caught the attention of local media. It sparked discussions about precognition, the nature of dreams, and whether our subconscious minds can glimpse future events.

For Michael, this experience was transformative. It not only led him to a new career but also opened his mind to the possibilities of intuition and foresight. He became an object of fascination among his coworkers, with many seeking his advice on their own dreams and career paths.

This remarkable tale of a dream job becoming a reality serves as a compelling example of life's unpredictable nature. It challenges our understanding of coincidence and causality, leaving us to ponder the mysterious ways in which our subconscious minds might shape our future paths.

Chapter Seventy-Three

The Duplicate Yearbook Photos: A Cross-Country Coincidence

In the vast landscape of American high schools, where millions of yearbook photos are taken each year, an extraordinary coincidence occurred that defies statistical probability. This is the story of two students, separated by thousands of miles, who discovered they had identical yearbook photos, creating a mystery that captivated the internet and left experts puzzled.

The tale begins with two high school seniors: Emma Richardson from a small town in Oregon, and Sophia Martinez from suburban Florida. In the spring of 2018, as yearbooks were distributed across the country, both girls eagerly flipped through the pages to find their senior portraits.

What they found left them in disbelief. Emma's friend was the first to notice, sending her a text message with a screenshot of a Florida high school's yearbook page that had gone viral on social media. There, staring back at Emma, was her exact yearbook photo – same pose, same outfit, same hairstyle, and even the same facial expression. But the name beneath the photo wasn't hers; it was Sophia Martinez.

Confused and intrigued, Emma reached out to Sophia through social media. The girls quickly confirmed that they were indeed different people, with no connection to each other. They had never met, had no mutual friends, and had taken their photos on different days in different studios thousands of miles apart.

As the girls shared their discovery online, the story quickly went viral. Internet sleuths analyzed every detail of the photos, confirming that they were indeed identical, down to the smallest elements. The coincidence seemed to defy explanation.

Theories began to circulate. Some suggested it must be an elaborate prank or a glitch in the yearbook printing process. Others proposed more far-fetched ideas, like parallel universes or long-lost twins separated at birth.

Photography experts weighed in, explaining that while school photographers often use similar poses and backdrops, the level of similarity in this case was unprecedented. The odds of two unrelated students in different states independently striking the exact same pose, with the same expression, hairstyle, and outfit, were astronomical.

The story caught the attention of national media, and soon Emma and Sophia found themselves at the center of a nationwide fascination. They appeared on morning shows, gave interviews, and became minor celebrities in their respective schools.

For Emma and Sophia, the experience was surreal. What started as a shocking discovery turned into an unexpected friendship. They began corresponding regularly, sharing the unique experience of being at the center of such an unusual coincidence.

The tale of the duplicate yearbook photos serves as a reminder of the incredible, often inexplicable coincidences that can occur in our interconnected world. It challenges our understanding of probability and leaves us to wonder about the hidden synchronicities that might be happening all around us, unnoticed.

This story continues to be cited in discussions about coincidence and probability, a testament to the enduring fascination we have with events that seem to defy logical explanation. It stands as a modern-day example of truth being stranger than fiction, reminding us that in a world of billions of people, the improbable becomes possible.

Chapter Seventy-Four

The Time Capsule Prediction: A Century-Old Vision of the Future

In the realm of historical predictions, few are as remarkably accurate as the contents of a time capsule buried in 1900 and opened a century later. This extraordinary case of foresight not only captured the imagination of the public but also raised intriguing questions about the nature of technological progress and human intuition.

The story begins in the final days of the 19th century. As the world stood on the brink of a new era, a group of forward-thinking individuals in a small Midwestern town decided to create a time capsule. Their goal was to preserve a snapshot of their time for future generations, but they also included something unusual – predictions for what life might be like in the year 2000.

The time capsule was sealed and buried beneath the cornerstone of the town hall, with instructions for it to be opened in 100 years. As the 20th century unfolded, the existence of the capsule was largely forgotten, becoming little more than a local legend.

When the year 2000 arrived, town officials remembered the century-old promise and organized an event to open the time capsule. As they unsealed the container and examined its contents, they found the usual artifacts of the era – newspapers, photographs, and small personal items. But it was a sealed envelope containing the predictions that truly captured everyone's attention.

To the astonishment of those present, many of the predictions were startlingly accurate. Among the most striking was a description of "wireless telephone and telegraph circuits," which bore an uncanny resemblance to modern mobile phones and wireless internet. The document also foresaw air travel becoming commonplace, homes being lit and heated by electricity, and the development of "horseless carriages" capable of high speeds.

Other predictions were even more specific. The author envisioned a world where information could be transmitted instantly across vast distances, where images could be sent over wires (akin to television and the internet), and where medical advancements would significantly extend human lifespans.

As news of these remarkably prescient predictions spread, it caught the attention of historians, technologists, and the media. Experts analyzed the language and content of the predictions, confirming their authenticity and marveling at their accuracy.

The story sparked discussions about the nature of technological progress and human foresight. Some saw it as evidence of the predictability of technological evolution, while others viewed it as an extraordinary case of intuition or even a form of accidental prophecy.

For the town, the time capsule became a source of pride and fascination, drawing visitors from around the world. It served as a tangible link between past and present, demonstrating both how far technology had come and how some visionaries of the past had glimpsed the shape of things to come.

This tale of the prophetic time capsule stands as a testament to human ingenuity and imagination. It reminds us that even in eras long past, there were those who could envision a future vastly different from their own time. The accuracy of these century-old predictions continues to inspire wonder and reflection on the pace of progress and the potential futures we might be shaping today.

Chapter Seventy-Five

The Synchronous Births: Sisters' Simultaneous Miracles

In the realm of familial connections, few stories are as extraordinary as that of the Thompson sisters, whose synchronized pregnancies and births defied astronomical odds. This tale of sisterly synchronicity spans continents and challenges our understanding of coincidence and biological rhythms.

Sarah and Emma Thompson, born just two years apart, had always been close despite the physical distance between them. Sarah had settled in Australia, while Emma made her home in Canada. In early 2015, both sisters discovered they were pregnant within weeks of each other, much to their mutual delight.

As their pregnancies progressed, the sisters kept in touch via video calls, sharing their experiences and marveling at the parallel journeys their bodies were undertaking. However, no one could have predicted the extraordinary event that was to unfold as their due dates approached.

On September 15, 2015, Sarah went into labor in Sydney. Halfway across the world in Vancouver, Emma's water broke at almost the exact same moment. Despite the 17-hour time difference between their locations, the sisters gave birth within minutes of each other.

The coincidences didn't end there. Both sisters delivered healthy baby girls, each weighing an identical 7 pounds, 3 ounces. The infants were born at 3:30 PM local time in their respective locations.

News of this extraordinary double birth quickly spread, first among family and friends, and then to local media. Medical professionals were astounded by the synchronicity, noting that the odds of such an occurrence – same day, same time (accounting for time zones), same gender, and same birth weight – were incredibly low.

Theories began to circulate about the possible explanations for this remarkable event. Some scientists suggested that the sisters' close genetic relationship might have played a role in synchronizing their biological clocks. Others proposed that their emotional closeness could have influenced their hormonal cycles.

The story captured the public's imagination, sparking discussions about the nature of sisterly bonds and the mysterious connections that can exist between twins or close siblings. It also raised intriguing questions about the potential for long-distance biological synchronization.

For Sarah and Emma, the simultaneous births created an even stronger bond between them and their daughters. The cousins, born at the same moment on opposite sides of the world, were affectionately dubbed "time-zone twins" by their families.

This tale of synchronous births serves as a powerful reminder of the deep connections that can exist within families, transcending distance and time. It challenges our understanding of coincidence and leaves us to ponder the mysterious ways in which human lives can align, even across vast distances.

The Thompson sisters' story continues to fascinate those who hear it, standing as a testament to the sometimes inexplicable synchronicities that can occur in our lives and the profound connections that bind us to our loved ones, no matter how far apart we may be.

Chapter Seventy-Six

The Reincarnation Reunion: A Child's Past-Life Memory

In the bustling state of Uttar Pradesh, India, a story unfolded that challenges our understanding of life, death, and the possibility of reincarnation. This extraordinary tale centers around a young boy named Akshay Tripathi, whose vivid memories of a past life led to a reunion that left many questioning the boundaries of consciousness and existence.

Akshay, from the age of three, began to speak about a life he claimed to have lived before. He described in detail a village he had never visited, a family he had never met, and experiences that seemed impossible for such a young child to know. His parents, initially skeptical, were astounded by the specificity and consistency of his claims.

The boy spoke of being a man named Rajesh Kumar, who had lived in a village some 100 kilometers away. He described his house, his occupation as a schoolteacher, and even the circumstances of his death – a motorcycle accident on a particular stretch of road.

Intrigued by Akshay's persistent claims, his family eventually decided to investigate. They traveled to the village Akshay had described, armed with the details he had provided. To their astonishment, they found the village exactly as Akshay had depicted it.

The most remarkable moment came when Akshay led them unerringly to a house he claimed was his former home. There, they encountered a family who confirmed that they had indeed lost a family member named Rajesh Kumar in a motorcycle accident several years prior, just before Akshay's birth.

What followed was a series of astonishing recognitions. Akshay identified family members by name, pointed out changes made to the house since "his" death, and even located possessions that had belonged to Rajesh, hidden in places only Rajesh would have known.

The case quickly gained attention, drawing researchers from the field of reincarnation studies. They meticulously documented Akshay's statements, verifying details that would have been impossible for him to know through normal means.

For Rajesh's family, the experience was both unsettling and comforting. While the idea of reincarnation challenged their beliefs, many found solace in the idea that their lost loved one had, in some form, returned.

Akshay's story is not unique in India, where belief in reincarnation is widespread. However, the level of detail and the verifiable nature of his memories make this case particularly compelling.

This extraordinary tale of past-life memories and reunion across lifetimes continues to fascinate those who encounter it. It raises profound questions about the nature of consciousness, the possibility of life after death, and the potential for memories to transcend physical existence.

Whether viewed as evidence of reincarnation or as an inexplicable psychological phenomenon, Akshay's story serves as a powerful reminder of the mysteries that still surround human consciousness and the enduring human quest to understand what lies beyond the boundaries of our known existence.

Chapter Seventy-Seven

The Prophetic Tattoo: Inked Numbers Lead to Fortune

In the realm of lottery wins and chance occurrences, few stories are as remarkably serendipitous as that of Daniel McCarthy, a man whose seemingly random tattoo led to an extraordinary stroke of luck. This tale of numerical coincidence challenges our understanding of chance and raises intriguing questions about fate and intuition.

Daniel, a 28-year-old graphic designer from Boston, had always been fascinated by numbers and their potential hidden meanings. In 2015, on a whim, he decided to get a tattoo of a sequence of numbers that had been recurring in his dreams: 7-15-23-31-36-44.

The tattoo artist was curious about the significance of these numbers, but Daniel simply shrugged, saying they felt important somehow. For the next few years, the tattoo was nothing more than an interesting conversation starter, a quirky piece of body art with a mysterious origin.

Fast forward to 2018. Daniel, who occasionally played the lottery, found himself standing in line at a convenience store. When it came time to fill out his ticket, he realized he hadn't thought of any numbers. In a split-second decision, he opted to use the numbers tattooed on his arm.

Days later, as the lottery drawing aired on television, Daniel watched in disbelief as the numbers were called: 7, 15, 23, 31, 36, and 44 – the exact sequence inked on his skin. He had won the jackpot, a sum of over $100 million.

News of Daniel's win, coupled with the story of his prophetic tattoo, quickly went viral. Media outlets clamored for interviews, and Daniel found himself thrust into the spotlight. People were fascinated by the idea that he had essentially been wearing the winning lottery numbers on his body for years.

The story sparked widespread discussion about premonitions, the nature of luck, and the potential for subconscious knowledge. Skeptics pointed out the astronomical odds against such a coincidence, suggesting there must be more to the story. Some even accused Daniel of fraud or of having insider information about the lottery.

Psychologists and parapsychologists weighed in, debating whether this could be a case of precognition or simply an extreme coincidence. The tattoo artist who had inked the numbers years earlier came forward, confirming Daniel's story and adding another layer of verification to the tale.

For Daniel, the experience was transformative. Beyond the financial windfall, it left him questioning the nature of reality and the potential power of intuition. He became an object of fascination, with many seeking him out for luck or insight into choosing lottery numbers.

This extraordinary tale of a prophetic tattoo leading to a lottery win serves as a captivating example of life's unpredictable nature. It challenges our understanding of coincidence and probability, leaving us to wonder about the potential for unconscious foresight and the mysterious ways in which information might be accessible to us.

Whether viewed as an incredible stroke of luck or something more mysterious, Daniel's story continues to intrigue and inspire, reminding us of the potential for extraordinary events in our seemingly ordinary lives.

Chapter Seventy-Eight

The Identical Strangers' Wedding: A Serendipitous Celebration

In the world of wedding planning, where couples strive for uniqueness, a remarkable coincidence occurred that brought two pairs of strangers together in the most unexpected way. This is the story of how two couples, unknown to each other, ended up having nearly identical weddings on the same day, at the same venue.

The tale begins with two couples: Emily and Michael from New York, and Sarah and James from New Jersey. Both pairs had independently fallen in love with a picturesque vineyard venue in upstate New York and booked it for their special day – June 15, 2019.

As the big day approached, both couples worked with their respective wedding planners, choosing decorations, color schemes, and other details to make their celebrations unique. Unbeknownst to them, their choices were aligning in an almost impossible way.

On the morning of June 15, as the two brides arrived at the venue to prepare, they were shocked to discover another wedding party setting up. Initially, there was confusion and concern about a double-booking.

However, as they began to compare notes, the true extent of the coincidence became apparent.

Not only had both couples chosen the same date and venue, but their wedding colors (blush pink and navy), flower arrangements (peonies and roses), and even the style of their wedding cakes (three-tier with metallic accents) were nearly identical. The similarities extended to their choice of music, with both hiring string quartets for the ceremony and selecting the same first dance song.

As guests began to arrive, they too were bewildered by the scene – two weddings, mirror images of each other, unfolding side by side. The coincidence was so striking that many initially thought it must be an elaborate prank or a set of twins having a double wedding.

What could have been a disaster instead turned into something magical. The two couples, struck by the humor and wonder of the situation, decided to embrace the coincidence. They introduced themselves to each other's guests, shared photographers, and even joined forces for some group photos.

The story quickly caught the attention of local media, with reporters rushing to cover this real-life "Parent Trap" scenario. Social media exploded with images and stories from guests, marveling at the serendipity of the event.

For Emily, Michael, Sarah, and James, what started as a potential wedding-day nightmare became an unforgettable experience that bonded them to complete strangers. They exchanged contact information and promised to celebrate their anniversaries together.

This tale of the identical strangers' wedding serves as a heartwarming reminder of the unpredictable nature of life and the joy that can come from embracing the unexpected. It challenges our notions of individuality and uniqueness, suggesting that even in our most personal moments, we may find surprising connections with others.

The story continues to be shared as an example of serendipity and the power of positive attitudes in the face of surprising circumstances. It stands as a testament to the idea that sometimes, the most memorable moments in life are the ones we never could have planned.

Chapter Seventy-Nine

The Time-Traveling Postcard: A Message from the Past

In an age of instant digital communication, the arrival of a physical postcard is already something of a novelty. But for Lisa Chen of San Francisco, the postcard that arrived in her mailbox in 2018 was more than just unusual – it was seemingly impossible.

The story begins on a typical Monday morning when Lisa, a 35-year-old software engineer, was sifting through her mail. Among the bills and advertisements was a colorful postcard that immediately caught her eye. The image on the front showed a vintage scene of San Francisco's Fisherman's Wharf, clearly from decades past.

But it was when Lisa turned the card over that her world turned upside down. The postcard was addressed to her grandmother, who had lived at Lisa's current address in the 1980s. The message was simple birthday wishes, signed by a family friend. What made Lisa's hair stand on end was the postmark: August 15, 1988 – precisely 30 years before the day it arrived in her mailbox.

Lisa's grandmother had passed away in 2010, making the arrival of this long-lost message even more poignant. The handwriting and content were unmistakably genuine, and the stamp was indeed from the 1980s.

Bewildered, Lisa contacted her local post office for an explanation. Postal workers were equally mystified. The card showed no signs of having been stuck in machinery or misplaced in a mail bag for three decades. It appeared to have simply materialized in the mail system, as fresh as the day it was sent.

As news of the time-traveling postcard spread, it captured the imagination of the public and media alike. Theories abounded: Had the card slipped through a wormhole in space-time? Was it proof of parallel universes? Or was there a more mundane explanation – perhaps a postal worker had found it in an old sorting bin and decided to finally deliver it?

Experts in postal history were consulted, and while they acknowledged that mail can sometimes be delayed for years due to clerical errors or being lost in the system, a delay of 30 years with the card arriving in pristine condition was unprecedented.

For Lisa, the experience was both eerie and deeply moving. The postcard provided an unexpected connection to her grandmother and a glimpse into a past she had never known. It sparked conversations with older family members, unearthing stories and memories that might otherwise have been lost to time.

The incident also reignited interest in physical mail in an increasingly digital world. Many were touched by the idea that a simple postcard could bridge decades, carrying a message from the past to the present.

This extraordinary tale of the time-traveling postcard serves as a reminder of the enduring power of written communication and the mysterious ways in which the past can sometimes reach out to touch the present. It stands as a testament to the unpredictable nature of life and the potential for wonder in the most unexpected places.

Whether explained as an elaborate postal mishap or something more mysterious, the story of Lisa's impossible postcard continues to intrigue and inspire, reminding us that even in our fast-paced modern world, there's still room for a little magic.

Chapter Eighty

The Synchronous Inventions: Simultaneous MRI Breakthroughs

In the annals of scientific discovery, few coincidences are as remarkable as the simultaneous invention of the Magnetic Resonance Imaging (MRI) machine in 1971. This extraordinary event, which occurred on opposite sides of the world, showcases the phenomenon of multiple discovery and the sometimes synchronous nature of human innovation.

The protagonists of this scientific serendipity were Dr. Raymond Damadian in the United States and Dr. Paul Lauterbur in the United Kingdom. Unbeknownst to each other, both scientists were working on similar principles that would eventually lead to the development of the MRI, a revolutionary medical imaging technique.

Dr. Damadian, working at Brooklyn's Downstate Medical Center, was exploring the potential of nuclear magnetic resonance (NMR) to distinguish between healthy and cancerous tissue. Meanwhile, across the Atlantic, Dr. Lauterbur at the University of Nottingham was investigating how to use NMR principles to create detailed images of the human body.

In a twist of fate that seems almost too coincidental to be true, both scientists made crucial breakthroughs in their research on the same day in July 1971. Damadian filed a patent for his "Apparatus and Method for Detecting Cancer in Tissue," while Lauterbur jotted down his ideas for using magnetic field gradients to create 2D images, a key principle of MRI technology.

Neither scientist was aware of the other's work at the time. It wasn't until later, when their findings were published and patents filed, that the scientific community realized the parallel nature of their discoveries.

This synchronicity in invention sparked discussions about the nature of scientific progress and the concept of "multiple discovery" – the hypothesis that most scientific discoveries and inventions are made independently and more or less simultaneously by multiple scientists.

The simultaneous invention of the MRI also led to controversies over credit and patents. Both Damadian and Lauterbur made significant contributions to the development of MRI technology, and debates over who should be considered the "true inventor" continued for years.

For the scientific community, this coincidence served as a powerful reminder of the collaborative nature of progress, even when that collaboration is unconscious. It highlighted how scientific advancements often occur when the time is ripe, with multiple minds converging on similar solutions to pressing problems.

The story of the synchronous invention of the MRI continues to fascinate scientists and historians alike. It stands as a testament to human ingenuity and the sometimes mysterious ways in which breakthrough ideas can emerge simultaneously in different parts of the world. This tale of coincidence in innovation reminds us that great ideas often transcend individual minds, emerging as part of a collective leap forward in human knowledge and capability.

Chapter Eighty-One

The Doppelgänger Encounter: Strangers on a Plane

In the vast world of air travel, where thousands of strangers cross paths daily, an extraordinary coincidence occurred that left passengers and flight crew alike in awe. This is the tale of two women, unrelated yet remarkably similar in appearance, who met by chance on a flight and discovered they shared more than just looks.

The incident took place on a routine flight from London to New York in 2015. As passengers boarded the plane, many did a double-take at two women who appeared to be identical twins. The women – let's call them Sarah and Emma – were equally shocked when they came face to face.

Sarah, taking her seat, found herself next to Emma. The resemblance was uncanny – same hair color and style, similar facial features, and even comparable fashion choices. Initially, both women assumed they must be related somehow, perhaps long-lost sisters or cousins.

As they began to chat, their astonishment grew. Not only did they look alike, but they also shared the same birthday – May 7th. However, Sarah was born in 1985 in London, while Emma was born in 1985 in New York. Despite the ocean between their birthplaces, they could have been mirror images of each other.

The coincidences didn't stop there. As their conversation deepened during the flight, they discovered more similarities. Both worked in marketing, enjoyed the same hobbies, and even had dogs of the same breed. Their mannerisms and speech patterns were so similar that other passengers began to take notice, creating a buzz of excitement throughout the plane.

By the time the flight landed in New York, news of the doppelgänger encounter had spread through the entire aircraft. Fellow passengers and crew members were fascinated, many taking photos of the lookalike pair. The story quickly made its way to social media and then to mainstream news outlets.

Geneticists and statisticians weighed in on the phenomenon, discussing the odds of such a coincidence. While it's not uncommon for unrelated people to share some physical traits, the degree of similarity between Sarah and Emma, coupled with their shared birthday and other commonalities, was deemed extraordinarily rare.

For Sarah and Emma, the chance encounter led to a unique friendship. They stayed in touch after the flight, marveling at their unlikely meeting and the bond it created. Their story sparked discussions about genetic diversity, the concept of doppelgängers, and the role of chance in human connections.

This tale of the doppelgänger encounter serves as a reminder of the unpredictable nature of life and the potential for extraordinary coincidences in the most ordinary of settings. It challenges our understanding of individuality and the factors that shape our appearances and personalities. The story of Sarah and Emma continues to captivate those who hear it, a testament to the enduring fascination we have with the idea of finding our double in the vast sea of humanity.

Chapter Eighty-Two

The Recurring Dream Location: A Prophetic Vision of Inheritance

In the mysterious realm of dreams, where the subconscious mind weaves intricate tapestries of imagery and emotion, a remarkable story unfolded that blurs the line between imagination and prophecy. This is the tale of Margaret Thornton, whose recurring dream of an unfamiliar house became an astonishing reality.

For years, Margaret, a 45-year-old librarian from Seattle, had been haunted by a vivid, recurring dream. In this dream, she would find herself exploring a distinctive Victorian-style house. The details were always the same: a wrap-around porch with intricate latticework, a unique stained-glass window above the front door, and a grand staircase with an ornate mahogany banister.

Night after night, Margaret would wander through the rooms of this dream house, marveling at its antique furnishings and the sense of history that permeated its walls. Despite the dream's regularity, she had never seen such a house in her waking life and had no idea why her subconscious had conjured such a specific and persistent image.

The dream remained a curious but seemingly meaningless aspect of Margaret's life until a fateful day in 2018. She received an unexpected call from a lawyer representing the estate of a great-aunt she had never met. To Margaret's shock, she was informed that this distant relative had passed away and left her sole heir to an estate – including a house – in a small town in Vermont.

When Margaret traveled to Vermont to see the property, she was stunned into silence. There, standing before her, was the exact house from her dreams. Every detail matched: the wrap-around porch, the stained-glass window, the grand staircase – all exactly as she had seen them in her sleep countless times.

As Margaret explored the house, she found herself navigating its layout with uncanny familiarity. She knew the location of hidden closets and could anticipate the views from each window. The experience was surreal, like walking through a dream in broad daylight.

News of Margaret's prophetic dreams and unexpected inheritance quickly spread, capturing the imagination of local media and then gaining national attention. Parapsychologists and dream researchers were intrigued, seeing it as a potential case of precognition or some form of inherited memory.

For Margaret, the experience was transformative. It challenged her understanding of reality and the potential power of dreams. She became fascinated with the history of the house and her unknown great-aunt, uncovering family stories and connections she had never known existed.

This extraordinary tale of a dream becoming reality serves as a compelling example of the mysteries that still surround human consciousness. It raises intriguing questions about the nature of time, the possibilities of precognition, and the potential for unknown connections between family members, even across generations.

Whether viewed as a remarkable coincidence, a case of subconscious knowledge, or something more mystical, Margaret's story continues to fascinate those who hear it. It stands as a testament to the sometimes prophetic nature of dreams and the surprising ways in which our lives can take unexpected turns, guided by visions we don't yet understand.

Chapter Eighty-Three

The Synchronous Heart Attacks: Twins' Cardiac Connection

In the realm of twin phenomena, few incidents are as startling and medically intriguing as the case of the Andersen twins, whose lives paralleled each other in the most extraordinary and potentially life-threatening way. This is the story of identical twins who, despite being separated by hundreds of miles, experienced simultaneous heart attacks, challenging our understanding of the bonds between twins and the mysteries of human physiology.

Jack and James Andersen, born in 1955, had always been close, sharing the unique bond often observed in identical twins. As adults, their lives had taken them to different parts of the country – Jack lived in Chicago, while James had settled in Atlanta, roughly 700 miles away. Despite the distance, they maintained regular contact and often joked about their continued similarity in tastes and habits.

On the morning of September 15, 2010, at precisely 9:17 AM Eastern Time, Jack experienced severe chest pain while at his office in Chicago. Recognizing the symptoms of a heart attack, his colleagues quickly called for an ambulance. At the exact same moment, 700 miles away in Atlanta, James was also struck with intense chest pain, collapsing at a job site where he worked as a construction foreman.

Both brothers were rushed to hospitals in their respective cities. In an astonishing twist of fate, they were both admitted at 9:45 AM local time, diagnosed with myocardial infarctions of surprisingly similar severity and location in the heart.

The medical teams treating the Andersen twins were baffled by the synchronicity of the events. As news of the coincidence spread between the families and eventually to the attending physicians, the case quickly became a subject of intense medical interest.

Cardiologists and geneticists were particularly intrigued. While it's well known that identical twins can have similar health predispositions, the timing and nature of these simultaneous heart attacks went beyond what medical science could easily explain.

Researchers began to investigate various theories. Some proposed that the twins' shared genetics and similar lifestyles might have predisposed them to heart issues that manifested at the same time. Others suggested more esoteric explanations, such as a deep physiological connection between twins that science has yet to fully understand.

For Jack and James, the experience was both frightening and affirming. It reinforced the unique bond they had always felt and sparked a joint commitment to improving their health. They recovered at similar rates and used their story to raise awareness about heart health, particularly among twins.

This case of synchronous heart attacks in distant twins serves as a fascinating example of the mysteries that still surround twin relationships. It challenges our understanding of the interplay between genetics, environment, and the possibly deeper connections that may exist between identical siblings.

The story of the Andersen twins continues to be discussed in medical circles and twin studies, a reminder of how much we have yet to learn about the human body and the profound connections that can exist between genetically identical individuals, regardless of distance.

Chapter Eighty-Four

The Time Slip Photo: A Captured Moment Across Decades

In the annals of unexplained phenomena, few incidents are as perplexing as the case of the Johnsons and their impossible photograph. This extraordinary event, which occurred in 2018, challenges our understanding of time and reality, leaving experts and laypeople alike searching for explanations.

Mark and Emily Johnson, a couple from Bristol, England, were on a weekend trip to Scotland, visiting historic castles. Their journey took them to Glamis Castle, a site steeped in history and legend. As they toured the castle grounds, Emily was struck by a feeling of déjà vu, as if she had been there before, though she knew she hadn't.

The couple decided to visit the castle's museum, which displayed historical artifacts and photographs. As they perused the exhibits, Mark suddenly froze in front of a black and white photograph dated 1968. He called Emily over, his voice trembling with disbelief.

The photograph showed a couple standing in front of the castle, and to the Johnsons' shock, they were the spitting image of Mark and Emily. Not only did the couple in the photo bear an uncanny resemblance to them, but they were wearing the exact same outfits that Mark and Emily had on that very day – down to Emily's distinctive floral scarf and Mark's vintage watch.

Stunned, the Johnsons approached the museum curator, who was equally baffled by the coincidence. The curator confirmed that the photograph had been part of the castle's collection for decades, its subjects unidentified but assumed to be visitors from 50 years ago.

News of this extraordinary coincidence quickly spread. Photographers and photography historians examined the image, confirming its age and authenticity. There was no doubt that the photograph was genuinely from 1968, yet it seemed to depict two people from 2018.

Theories abounded. Some suggested a remarkable case of genetic throwback, where the Johnsons happened to look exactly like and dress similarly to a couple from decades past. Others proposed more fantastic explanations, like time travel or parallel universes.

The incident attracted the attention of paranormal researchers, who interviewed the Johnsons and conducted investigations at the castle. While they found no definitive explanations, many were intrigued by Emily's feeling of déjà vu, wondering if it might be connected to the phenomenon.

For Mark and Emily, the experience was profound and unsettling. They found themselves questioning the nature of reality and time. The incident sparked a deep interest in the castle's history and the couple in the photograph, leading them to embark on a quest to uncover more information.

This case of the time slip photo stands as one of the most puzzling incidents in the realm of unexplained phenomena. It continues to captivate the imagination of many, challenging our understanding of time, coincidence, and the mysteries that can unfold in seemingly ordinary moments. Whether a remarkable coincidence or something more, the Johnsons' experience at Glamis Castle remains a fascinating enigma, a moment where past and present seemed to converge in a single, impossible photograph.

Chapter Eighty-Five

The Prophetic Novel: Poe's Grim Foreshadowing

In the annals of literary prophecy, few instances are as chilling and precise as the case of Edgar Allan Poe's only complete novel, "The Narrative of Arthur Gordon Pym of Nantucket." Published in 1838, this work of fiction would, nearly half a century later, foreshadow a gruesome real-life event with uncanny accuracy.

Poe's novel tells the tale of four survivors of a shipwreck who, adrift in a small boat and facing starvation, resort to cannibalism. In the story, the men draw lots to decide who will be sacrificed to feed the others. The unfortunate victim is a young cabin boy named Richard Parker.

Fast forward to 1884, when a real shipwreck occurred that would mirror Poe's fiction in disturbingly similar detail. The Mignonette, an English yacht, sank in a storm while sailing from Southampton to Australia. Four crew members survived the initial disaster: Captain Tom Dudley, mate Edwin Stephens, sailor Edmund Brooks, and a 17-year-old cabin boy named Richard Parker.

For 19 days, the four men drifted in a small lifeboat, their supplies dwindling rapidly. Faced with imminent starvation, Captain Dudley proposed that one of them should be sacrificed to save the others. The desperate crew decided that Parker, who had fallen ill after drinking seawater, should be the one to die.

The parallels between Poe's novel and the Mignonette tragedy are striking. Not only did both stories involve shipwreck survivors resorting to cannibalism, but in both cases, the victim was named Richard Parker. The real Parker, like his fictional counterpart, was indeed the youngest and most vulnerable member of the crew.

When the surviving crew members of the Mignonette were rescued and returned to England, they faced trial for murder. The case became a landmark in English common law, known as R v Dudley and Stephens, which established that necessity is not a defense for murder.

The eerie similarities between Poe's novel and the Mignonette incident did not go unnoticed. Literary scholars and coincidence enthusiasts were quick to point out the parallels, sparking discussions about the nature of prophecy in literature and the sometimes uncanny ability of fiction to prefigure reality.

Some saw it as evidence of Poe's almost supernatural foresight, while others viewed it as a remarkable but ultimately explicable coincidence. Skeptics pointed out that shipwrecks and survival cannibalism were not uncommon topics in 19th-century literature and maritime lore.

Regardless of how one interprets it, the case of Poe's prophetic novel remains one of the most striking examples of life imitating art. It continues to fascinate readers and scholars alike, serving as a grim reminder of the thin line between fiction and reality, and the sometimes prophetic power of the literary imagination.

Chapter Eighty-Six

The Time-Traveling Bullet: A Civil War Message Preserved

In 2010, a remarkable discovery in the forests of Virginia bridged a 147-year gap in time, connecting the present day with one of the most tumultuous periods in American history. This extraordinary find came in the form of a Civil War bullet, but it was what the bullet contained that truly captured the imagination of historians and the public alike.

The story begins with a group of Civil War enthusiasts using metal detectors to search for artifacts in an area known to have been a battleground. One of the searchers, John Williamson, received a strong signal from his device. Upon digging, he unearthed what appeared to be a standard bullet from the Civil War era.

However, as Williamson examined the bullet more closely, he noticed something unusual. The lead casing seemed to have been carefully hollowed out and resealed. Intrigued, he gently pried it open, revealing a tightly rolled piece of paper inside.

To Williamson's astonishment, the paper contained a legible message written in pencil. The note was dated June 30, 1863, just days before the Battle of Gettysburg. It read: "Dear Mother, The fight is coming. I may not make it home. I love you. Your son, William."

The discovery sent shockwaves through the historical community. Here was a personal message from a Civil War soldier, preserved for nearly a century and a half within the very instrument of war that might have taken his life. The bullet had effectively served as a time capsule, protecting the soldier's last words from the ravages of time.

Experts were called in to authenticate the find. They confirmed that both the bullet and the paper were consistent with materials from the Civil War era. Handwriting analysts studied the penmanship, while historians worked to identify the soldier based on military records from the time.

The story quickly captured public interest, spreading from local news to national media. Many were touched by the personal nature of the message, seeing it as a poignant reminder of the individual human stories behind the grand narratives of history.

For historians, the discovery offered a rare, intimate glimpse into the mindset of a soldier on the eve of one of the war's most significant battles. It provided valuable insights into the emotional state of combatants and the ways they sought to communicate with loved ones in their final moments.

The bullet and its message were eventually donated to a museum, where they continue to serve as a powerful exhibit, bridging the gap between past and present. The discovery serves as a reminder of the countless untold stories that lie hidden in the artifacts of history, waiting to be uncovered.

This extraordinary find, dubbed the "time-traveling bullet" by some, stands as a testament to the enduring power of human connection across time. It reminds us that even in the midst of great historical events, individual hopes, fears, and love persist, sometimes preserved in the most unlikely of places.

Chapter Eighty-Seven

The Synchronous Discoveries: Gallium's Dual Birth

In the annals of scientific discovery, few coincidences are as striking as the simultaneous identification of the element gallium by two chemists working independently on opposite sides of Europe. This remarkable event, which occurred in 1875, serves as a classic example of simultaneous discovery in science and highlights the sometimes synchronous nature of human innovation.

The protagonists of this scientific serendipity were Paul-Émile Lecoq de Boisbaudran, a French chemist, and Dmitri Mendeleev, a Russian chemist best known for his work on the periodic table of elements. Unbeknownst to each other, both scientists were working on identifying new elements to fill gaps in the periodic table.

On August 20, 1875, Lecoq de Boisbaudran discovered a new element through spectroscopic analysis of a zinc blende sample from the Pyrenees. He named this new element "gallia," after Gaul, the ancient name for France. On the very same day, thousands of miles away in St. Petersburg, Mendeleev independently predicted the existence of the same element, which he called "eka-aluminum" based on its position in his periodic table.

The synchronicity of these discoveries is made even more remarkable by the fact that the two scientists employed different methods. Lecoq de Boisbaudran's discovery was experimental, based on observational data, while Mendeleev's was theoretical, derived from his work on the periodic law.

When news of the dual discovery spread through the scientific community, it caused quite a stir. The simultaneous nature of the find raised fascinating questions about the nature of scientific discovery and the concept of scientific zeitgeist - the idea that certain discoveries become almost inevitable when the collective knowledge of the scientific community reaches a certain point.

The gallium coincidence also sparked discussions about priority in scientific discoveries. In this case, both Lecoq de Boisbaudran and Mendeleev received credit for their work. Lecoq de Boisbaudran was recognized for the physical discovery and isolation of the element, while Mendeleev was credited for its theoretical prediction.

This incident served as a powerful validation of Mendeleev's periodic table and his method of predicting the properties of undiscovered elements. It demonstrated the predictive power of good scientific theories and helped to cement the periodic table's place as a cornerstone of chemistry.

The story of gallium's dual discovery continues to be cited in discussions about the nature of scientific progress and the phenomenon of multiple discovery. It stands as a testament to the sometimes mysterious ways in which human knowledge advances, with great minds often arriving at the same conclusions independently and simultaneously.

This remarkable coincidence in the history of chemistry serves as a reminder of the collaborative nature of scientific progress, even when that collaboration is unconscious. It highlights how scientific advancements often occur when the time is ripe, with multiple researchers converging on similar discoveries, guided by the accumulated knowledge and methodologies of their field.

Chapter Eighty-Eight

The Prophetic Arcade Game: Pixels Predict Baseball History

In the intersection of pop culture and sports, few coincidences are as fascinating as the case of a 1981 Japanese arcade game that seemingly predicted the outcome of a major baseball game three years into the future. This extraordinary event blurs the lines between chance, prophecy, and the sometimes mysterious ways in which reality can mirror fiction.

The story centers around a baseball-themed arcade game released in Japan in 1981. The game, while popular, was fairly standard for its time, allowing players to control a baseball team through a season. However, one particular detail in the game would later prove to be remarkably prescient.

In the game's final championship match, players faced a computer-controlled team. If the player won, they were treated to an end screen showing the score of their victory. What no one realized at the time was that this seemingly random score would foreshadow a real-life baseball outcome years later.

Fast forward to October 1984. In Game 5 of the Japan Series (the Japanese equivalent of the World Series), the Hiroshima Toyo Carp faced off against the Hankyu Braves. In a surprising turn of events, the Carp defeated the Braves with a score of 6-2, clinching the series.

What made this outcome extraordinary was that it exactly matched the score displayed in the end screen of the 1981 arcade game, right down to the specific teams involved. The game had, three years earlier, predicted not only the correct score but also the correct teams in their correct positions (winner and loser).

When this coincidence was discovered, it caused a sensation in Japan. Baseball fans, gamers, and statisticians alike were astounded by the precision of this apparent prophecy. The story quickly spread, first through gaming and sports circles, and then to mainstream media.

Experts were consulted to calculate the odds of such a prediction coming true. Considering the specific teams, the exact score, and the championship context, the probability was deemed astronomically low. This led to much speculation about the nature of coincidence and prediction.

Some saw it as evidence of the game developers having some sort of prophetic insight. Others viewed it as an extreme example of life imitating art. Skeptics pointed out that given the vast number of video games and sporting events that occur, some coincidences are bound to happen eventually.

For the gaming community, this incident became a part of industry lore, often cited as one of the most remarkable coincidences in video game history. It added a layer of mystique to the early days of arcade gaming and sparked discussions about the potential for games to inadvertently predict future events.

This tale of the prophetic arcade game serves as a fascinating example of the unexpected ways in which different aspects of culture can intersect. It highlights our human fascination with prediction and coincidence, and the excitement we feel when the improbable becomes reality. Whether viewed as mere chance or something more mysterious, the story continues to captivate those who hear it, a pixelated prophecy that briefly united the worlds of gaming and baseball in an extraordinary moment of synchronicity.

Chapter Eighty-Nine

The Identical Strangers' Career: A Life in Parallel

In the realm of coincidences, few stories are as striking as that of John Smith from England and Juan Smythe from Argentina. Their tale of parallel lives, discovered by chance, challenges our understanding of randomness and the factors that shape our life paths.

Born on May 15, 1970, John in London and Juan in Buenos Aires had no knowledge of each other's existence for most of their lives. It wasn't until 2015, when both men were 45, that their paths crossed virtually through a work-related international conference call.

The initial shock came when they realized they shared the same birthday. But as they began to chat, the coincidences multiplied at an astonishing rate. Both John and Juan had pursued careers in marketing, specializing in digital advertising. Remarkably, they both worked for companies named "Phoenix Digital" - John for the UK branch and Juan for the South American division, though the companies were unrelated despite the identical names.

The parallels didn't end there. When discussing their personal lives, they discovered that both were married to women named Sarah. Both had two children - a boy and a girl - and both owned golden retrievers as family pets.

As news of these extraordinary coincidences spread among their colleagues, John and Juan began to delve deeper into their histories. They found that they had both studied marketing at university, graduated in 1992, and started their first jobs at local advertising agencies on the same date.

The story quickly caught media attention, first locally, then internationally. Statisticians were consulted to calculate the odds of such extensive parallels, concluding that they were astronomically low. Psychologists and sociologists weighed in, discussing the interplay of choice, cultural influences, and chance in shaping life paths.

For John and Juan, the discovery was both fascinating and unsettling. They formed a friendship, regularly communicating to compare notes on their lives. Their families were equally intrigued, with the children particularly amused by their "international twins."

This case of identical strangers became a topic of much discussion in various fields. It challenged notions of individual uniqueness and raised questions about the degree to which our lives are shaped by factors beyond our control. Some saw it as evidence of a hidden order in the universe, while others viewed it as an extreme case of coincidence.

The story of John and Juan serves as a remarkable example of how lives can mirror each other across vast distances. It reminds us of the complex interplay of choice, chance, and circumstance in shaping our journeys through life. Their parallel careers and personal lives continue to fascinate those who hear about them, offering a glimpse into the mysterious ways in which human lives can align, even across continental divides.

Chapter Ninety

The Prophetic Song Lyrics: A Musical Premonition of 9/11

In the realm of eerie coincidences, few are as chilling as the case of a 1960s folk song that seemed to predict the events of September 11, 2001, with uncanny accuracy. This extraordinary example of apparent pre-science has fascinated and disturbed people in equal measure, raising questions about the nature of prophecy and the sometimes mysterious ways in which art can foreshadow reality.

The song in question, "The Man Who Saw Tomorrow," was written by folk singer John Stewart in 1967. Stewart, known for his work with the Kingston Trio, penned the lyrics as part of a larger collection of songs about American life and culture. At the time, the song was noted for its haunting melody and cryptic lyrics but didn't receive particular attention.

However, in the aftermath of the 9/11 attacks, the song resurfaced, and listeners were struck by the apparent parallels between its lyrics and the tragic events that unfolded on that September morning. The most striking lines included references to "metal birds" falling from the sky and crashing into tall buildings in New York City, as well as mentioning the month of September specifically.

When the coincidence was discovered, it sent shockwaves through the music community and beyond. Many were astounded by the specificity of the imagery that seemed to align so closely with the 9/11 attacks, despite being written over three decades earlier.

Skeptics argued that the lyrics were vague enough to be interpreted in multiple ways and that the apparent prophecy was a case of retrospective interpretation. They pointed out that fears of attacks on New York City had been a part of the cultural consciousness for many years.

Others saw the song as evidence of some form of precognition or prophetic ability. Parapsychologists and those interested in supernatural phenomena viewed it as a potential case of an artist unknowingly tapping into future events.

For his part, John Stewart (who passed away in 2008) was reportedly unsettled by the connections drawn between his song and the 9/11 attacks. In interviews given after 2001, he stated that he had no explanation for the apparent prophecy and that the lyrics had come to him as part of his creative process without any sense of their potential future significance.

The story of "The Man Who Saw Tomorrow" sparked widespread discussions about the nature of artistic inspiration and the potential for unconscious foresight. It led to renewed interest in other cases of apparent prophecies in art and literature, with many combing through works of the past for other potential predictions.

This incident serves as a powerful reminder of the sometimes mysterious nature of creativity and the human tendency to find patterns and meaning in coincidence. Whether viewed as a remarkable case of unintentional prophecy or simply an extraordinary coincidence, the story of this prescient folk song continues to intrigue and unsettle those who encounter it.

It stands as a testament to the enduring power of art to resonate across time, sometimes in ways that its creators could never have anticipated, and the complex relationship between creative expression and the events that shape our world.

Chapter Ninety-One

The Reincarnation Languages: A Boy's Ancient Greek Mystery

In the realm of reincarnation stories, few are as compelling and well-documented as the case of a young American boy who spontaneously began speaking fluent ancient Greek. This extraordinary incident, which occurred in the early 2000s, challenged conventional explanations and sparked intense debate in both scientific and spiritual communities.

The story centers around Alex Jones (name changed for privacy), a five-year-old boy from a small town in Ohio. Alex came from a typical American family with no Greek heritage or exposure to the Greek language, ancient or modern. His parents were startled when, seemingly overnight, Alex began speaking in a language they couldn't understand.

Initially thinking it was mere gibberish, Alex's parents became increasingly puzzled as their son continued to speak consistently in this unknown tongue. It wasn't until they consulted a linguist that the true nature of Alex's speech was revealed: he was speaking fluent ancient Greek, specifically a dialect from the Hellenistic period (323 BC to 31 BC).

What made this case particularly intriguing was not just Alex's ability to speak the language, but his claim that he was remembering a past life in ancient Greece. He provided detailed descriptions of life in a Greek city-state, including specific information about daily routines, religious practices, and historical events that a modern child would have no way of knowing.

The case attracted the attention of researchers in various fields. Linguists were amazed by Alex's command of a dead language, while historians found his accounts of ancient Greek life to be remarkably accurate, often including details that were not common knowledge but were verifiable through academic sources.

Skeptics proposed various explanations, from an elaborate hoax to cryptomnesia (the emergence of memories acquired in ways the individual cannot recall). However, extensive investigations, including psychological evaluations and background checks, found no evidence to support these theories.

For those who believe in reincarnation, Alex's case became a powerful piece of evidence. They argued that his detailed knowledge and linguistic abilities could only be explained by memories carried over from a past life. The specificity of his recollections, they claimed, went far beyond what could be attributed to chance or subconscious learning.

The scientific community, while generally skeptical of reincarnation claims, found the case intriguing enough to warrant serious study. Researchers in cognitive science and neurolinguistics were particularly interested in understanding how a young child could acquire such complex language skills seemingly out of nowhere.

As Alex grew older, his abilities in ancient Greek remained, though his memories of the "past life" gradually faded. He went on to become a subject of numerous studies and documentaries, his case continuing to provoke discussion and debate.

This extraordinary instance of apparent xenoglossy (the ability to speak a language one has never learned) and past-life recall stands as one of the most puzzling cases in the study of reincarnation and consciousness. It challenges our understanding of language acquisition, memory, and the nature of human consciousness itself.

Whether viewed as evidence of reincarnation or as an as-yet-unexplained phenomenon of the human mind, Alex's story continues to fascinate those who encounter it, serving as a reminder of the mysteries that still surround human consciousness and the potential depths of our cognitive abilities.

Chapter Ninety-Two

The Synchronous Scientific Papers: A Parallel Discovery

In the world of scientific research, where originality and priority are paramount, the case of Dr. Emily Chen and Dr. Hans Mueller stands out as an extraordinary example of simultaneous discovery. This remarkable incident, which occurred in 2015, challenges our understanding of how scientific breakthroughs occur and highlights the sometimes synchronous nature of human innovation.

Dr. Chen, a biochemist at Stanford University, and Dr. Mueller, a researcher at the Max Planck Institute in Germany, were working independently on the problem of protein folding, a crucial area in understanding diseases like Alzheimer's. Unknown to each other, they had been pursuing similar lines of inquiry for years.

On May 15, 2015, both scientists submitted papers to different prestigious journals - Chen to "Nature" and Mueller to "Science." The papers outlined nearly identical methods for predicting protein structures using machine learning algorithms. The similarity wasn't just in the general approach; even specific mathematical formulas and experimental designs were remarkably alike.

The coincidence came to light during the peer review process when a reviewer for "Science" noticed the striking similarities to Chen's paper, which he had reviewed for "Nature" just days earlier. Initially suspecting plagiarism, the journals launched investigations.

What they uncovered was astonishing. There was no evidence of communication between Chen and Mueller, no shared conferences, no common collaborators. They had arrived at the same groundbreaking conclusions independently, their research paths converging in a moment of scientific serendipity.

The scientific community was abuzz with discussion. Some saw it as a classic case of multiple discovery, akin to the simultaneous development of calculus by Newton and Leibniz. Others viewed it as evidence of a 'zeitgeist' in science, where global research conditions make certain discoveries almost inevitable.

For Chen and Mueller, the discovery was both exciting and unsettling. They quickly established contact, comparing notes and marveling at the parallels in their work. What could have been a contentious priority dispute instead became a collaboration, with the two deciding to publish a joint paper combining their findings.

This incident sparked debates about the nature of scientific discovery and the role of individual genius versus collective progress. It challenged the traditional narrative of the lone scientist making breakthroughs in isolation.

The Chen-Mueller case has since become a textbook example in the philosophy of science, illustrating how scientific progress often occurs in parallel across the globe. It serves as a reminder of the interconnected nature of modern research and the sometimes mysterious ways in which human minds, working independently, can arrive at the same innovations simultaneously.

This remarkable coincidence in biochemistry not only advanced our understanding of protein folding but also provided valuable insights into the process of scientific discovery itself, highlighting the complex interplay of individual brilliance and the collective scientific endeavor.

Chapter Ninety-Three

The Prophetic TV Show: A Western's Uncanny Political Foreshadowing

In the annals of pop culture prophecy, few instances are as striking as the case of a 1958 Western television series that seemed to predict a significant political figure and policy nearly 60 years into the future. This remarkable coincidence has fascinated TV historians and political commentators alike, sparking discussions about the cyclical nature of history and the sometimes prescient power of fiction.

The television show in question was "Trackdown," a CBS Western series that aired from 1957 to 1959. In an episode titled "The End of the World," which aired on May 9, 1958, the plot revolved around a conman named Walter Trump who arrives in a small town, claiming that only he can prevent the end of the world by building a wall around the town.

The similarities to future events are uncanny. The character's surname, Trump, matches that of Donald Trump, who would become the 45th President of the United States in 2017. Moreover, the fictional Trump's promise to build a wall eerily mirrors one of the real Donald Trump's key campaign promises - to build a wall along the U.S.-Mexico border.

When this coincidence was discovered during the 2016 U.S. presidential campaign, it quickly went viral. Clips from the episode circulated widely on social media, leaving many viewers astounded by the parallels. The show's Trump character even uses phrases reminiscent of the real Trump's rhetorical style, further adding to the sense of prophecy.

Skeptics were quick to point out that "Trump" is not an uncommon surname and that the idea of building walls for protection is an age-old concept. They argued that the similarities were merely a coincidence amplified by confirmation bias. However, the specificity of the name combined with the wall-building promise struck many as too precise to be mere chance.

The incident sparked discussions about the nature of political cycles and the recurrence of certain themes in American culture. Some commentators saw it as an example of how certain political ideas and personality types tend to resurface periodically in American history.

For TV historians, the "Trackdown" episode became a subject of intense interest. It led to broader examinations of how past television shows may have inadvertently predicted or influenced future events. The incident also reignited interest in other cases of apparent pop culture prophecy, with people combing through old shows and movies for other potential predictions.

This case of the prophetic TV show serves as a fascinating example of life imitating art – or perhaps art unknowingly foreshadowing life. It challenges our understanding of coincidence and raises intriguing questions about the relationship between popular culture and political reality.

Whether viewed as an extraordinary coincidence or a case of history rhyming, the story of "Trackdown" and its Trump character continues to captivate those who encounter it. It stands as a testament to the sometimes mysterious ways in which fiction can seem to reach across time, offering glimpses of a future its creators could never have imagined.

Chapter Ninety-Four

The Identical Strangers' Deaths: A Tale of Uncanny Parallels

In the realm of coincidences, few stories are as eerily symmetrical as the case of John William Smith and James William Smith, two men whose lives and deaths aligned in ways that defy statistical probability. This extraordinary tale of parallel destinies unfolded in 2002, leaving families, medical professionals, and statisticians in awe of the synchronicities involved.

John William Smith was born on March 13, 1940, in Austin, Texas. On the very same day, thousands of miles away in Baton Rouge, Louisiana, James William Smith entered the world. Both boys were given their names independently by their parents, with no knowledge of each other's existence.

Throughout their lives, the two men lived entirely separate existences, never crossing paths. John became a teacher in Dallas, while James pursued a career in accounting in New Orleans. Both married, had children, and led typical middle-class American lives.

The truly astonishing part of their story, however, came at the end of their lives. On July 21, 2002, both John and James died. They were both

62 years old. But the coincidences didn't stop there. John passed away at St. David's Hospital in Austin, while James took his last breath at St. Joseph's Hospital in Baton Rouge. Both men succumbed to heart attacks, and both were pronounced dead at 12:42 PM local time.

When the families of John and James learned of these extraordinary parallels, they were stunned. The coincidence was so precise and multi-faceted that it seemed to defy logical explanation. Statisticians calculated the odds of such an occurrence – two unrelated men with the same name, born on the same day, dying on the same day at the same age, in hospitals with the same name in different states – as astronomically low.

The case quickly garnered media attention, first locally and then nationally. It sparked discussions among scientists, philosophers, and the general public about the nature of coincidence, fate, and the possible hidden connections in human lives.

Researchers delved into the men's backgrounds, searching for any hidden links that might explain the synchronicity, but found none. Genetic tests confirmed that they were not related. The families, initially strangers to each other, formed a bond over their shared extraordinary experience.

This incident challenged many people's understanding of probability and raised questions about the existence of underlying patterns in the universe that we may not yet comprehend. Some saw it as evidence of a grand design, while others viewed it as an extreme example of the law of large numbers – given enough people and enough time, even the most improbable coincidences will occur.

The story of John and James Smith serves as a powerful reminder of the mysterious ways in which human lives can align. It continues to fascinate those who hear it, standing as one of the most striking examples of coincidence in recorded history. Their parallel lives and deaths remain a subject of wonder, a testament to the unpredictable and sometimes inexplicable nature of human existence.

Chapter Ninety-Five

The Time Capsule Photograph: A Face from the Past

In 2015, the small town of Millbrook, New Hampshire, became the center of an extraordinary coincidence that blurred the lines between past and present. This remarkable event unfolded during the opening of a time capsule, buried a century earlier, which contained a photograph that seemed to defy the laws of time and genetics.

The time capsule, a sturdy metal box, was unearthed as part of Millbrook's bicentennial celebrations. It had been buried in 1915 by the town's founders with instructions to be opened 100 years later. As town officials carefully extracted the contents, they found the usual artifacts of the era - newspapers, coins, and various documents. However, it was a particular photograph that caught everyone's attention and would soon capture the imagination of the entire town and beyond.

The sepia-toned image showed a group of men standing in front of the old town hall. One man, standing slightly apart from the others, bore an uncanny resemblance to Michael Henderson, a current resident of Millbrook. The likeness was so striking that many initially thought it was a prank - that somehow a modern photo of Michael had been slipped into the capsule.

However, authentication experts quickly confirmed the photograph's age and origin. It was, indeed, a genuine artifact from 1915. The man in the photo wasn't Michael Henderson, but the resemblance was undeniable - same strong jawline, distinctive nose, and even the same slight tilt of the head.

As news of this discovery spread, Michael Henderson became the center of attention. He had no known relatives from that era in Millbrook, having moved to the town only a decade ago. Genealogists and local historians scrambled to find a connection between Michael and the man in the photo but came up empty-handed.

The coincidence sparked widespread fascination. Some saw it as evidence of reincarnation, while others speculated about long-lost family connections. Scientists discussed the possibilities of genetic throwbacks and the recurrence of physical traits across unrelated lineages.

For Michael, the experience was surreal. He found himself staring at an image that could have been his own reflection, yet it was a man who had lived and died long before he was born. The incident prompted him to delve into his family history, uncovering stories and connections he had never known before.

The town of Millbrook embraced the mystery. The photograph became a local attraction, drawing visitors from far and wide. It sparked a renewed interest in local history, with many residents digging into their own family archives, searching for other hidden connections to the past.

This extraordinary coincidence serves as a powerful reminder of the mysterious ways in which the past can echo into the present. It challenges our understanding of time, genetics, and the connections that bind us across generations. The Millbrook time capsule photograph stands as a testament to the enduring fascination we have with our roots and the sometimes inexplicable links that can emerge between past and present.

Whether viewed as a remarkable coincidence or something more mysterious, the story of the Millbrook doppelganger continues to captivate those who hear it, a moment where history seemed to reach out and touch the present in the most personal and visual of ways.

Chapter Ninety-Six

The Synchronous Space Discoveries: A Cosmic Coincidence

In the vast expanse of the night sky, where countless celestial bodies move in their eternal dance, a remarkable coincidence occurred that highlighted the shared passion and keen eyes of amateur astronomers across the globe. This is the story of how two stargazers, separated by thousands of miles, simultaneously made the same groundbreaking discovery.

On the night of September 15, 2017, the stars aligned in more ways than one for Maria Sánchez in Chile and Hiroshi Tanaka in Japan. Both were amateur astronomers with a deep love for the cosmos, spending their free time scanning the skies with their home telescopes. Little did they know that this ordinary night would lead to an extraordinary coincidence.

At precisely 22:14 UTC, Maria, from her backyard observatory in Santiago, spotted a faint smudge of light that didn't appear on any of her star charts. Excited by the potential discovery, she began to document her observation, meticulously recording the object's position and characteristics.

At that exact same moment, halfway across the world in Osaka, Hiroshi's keen eye caught the same anomaly. He too recognized it as something new and potentially significant, and began his own process of verification and documentation.

Unaware of each other's discovery, both Maria and Hiroshi submitted their findings to the Minor Planet Center, the official world repository for such observations. When the center received two reports of the same comet, logged at the exact same time from observers on opposite sides of the planet, it caused quite a stir in the astronomical community.

The comet, later officially named C/2017 S1, became known colloquially as the "Synchronicity Comet" among astronomers. The odds of two amateur astronomers spotting the same previously undiscovered comet at precisely the same moment were astronomical, pardon the pun.

This coincidence sparked discussions about the nature of scientific discovery and the valuable contributions of amateur astronomers to the field. It highlighted how, in the age of global communication and shared passion, breakthroughs can occur simultaneously across vast distances.

For Maria and Hiroshi, this serendipitous event led to an unexpected friendship. They began corresponding regularly, sharing their love for astronomy and the night sky. Their story inspired many other amateur astronomers, showing that anyone with passion and perseverance could make significant contributions to our understanding of the universe.

The tale of the Synchronicity Comet serves as a beautiful reminder of how science can bring people together across cultural and geographical boundaries. It stands as a testament to the universal human desire to explore and understand the cosmos, and the magical moments that can occur when dedicated individuals, no matter where they are, look up at the same sky with wonder and curiosity.

This cosmic coincidence continues to be celebrated in astronomical circles, a cherished example of how the vastness of space can sometimes make our world feel smaller, connecting us in the most unexpected and delightful ways.

Chapter Ninety-Seven

The Mirrored Lottery Tickets: A Numerical Palindrome

In the world of lottery coincidences, few stories are as mathematically intriguing as the case of the mirrored lottery tickets that occurred in a small town in Idaho in 2019. This extraordinary event not only defied astronomical odds but also created a fascinating numerical palindrome that left mathematicians and probability experts in awe.

The story begins with two neighbors, let's call them John and Sarah, who lived on opposite sides of Elm Street in the quiet town of Millbrook, Idaho. On a whim, both decided to purchase lottery tickets for the state draw on the same day, unbeknownst to each other.

When the lottery results were announced, the town of Millbrook was buzzing with excitement. Both John and Sarah had won significant prizes, but it was the nature of their winning numbers that truly captured everyone's attention.

John's winning numbers were 13-24-35-46-57, while Sarah's ticket showed 75-64-53-42-31. At first glance, these might seem like random sequences, but upon closer inspection, it became clear that the two sets of numbers were exact mirror images of each other.

The odds of two neighbors winning the lottery on the same day with mirrored numbers are so astronomically low that statisticians struggled to calculate them accurately. Some experts estimated the probability to be in the billions to one.

News of this mathematical marvel spread quickly, first through local media and then gaining national attention. Mathematicians and numerologists flocked to Millbrook, eager to study this real-world example of numerical symmetry.

The coincidence sparked discussions about the nature of randomness and the hidden patterns that might exist in seemingly chaotic systems. Some saw it as evidence of an underlying order in the universe, while others viewed it as an extreme example of chance.

For John and Sarah, the win was life-changing in more ways than one. Beyond the financial windfall, they found themselves at the center of a probability phenomenon that would be studied for years to come. Their story became a favorite anecdote in mathematics classes, used to illustrate concepts of symmetry and the surprising ways numbers can align.

This incredible lottery coincidence serves as a reminder of the unpredictable nature of chance and the fascinating patterns that can emerge from randomness. It stands as a testament to the idea that in a world governed by probabilities, even the most improbable events can sometimes occur, creating moments of wonder that challenge our understanding of the laws of chance.

Chapter Ninety-Eight

The Telepathic Twins' Rescue: A Synchronized Saving

In 2008, a remarkable event unfolded in the Australian outback that would challenge our understanding of twin connections and intuition. This is the story of Emma and Olivia Thompson, identical twins whose inexplicable bond led to a lifesaving rescue that defies conventional explanation.

On a seemingly ordinary Tuesday afternoon, Emma, who lived in Sydney, suddenly experienced an overwhelming panic attack. At the exact same moment, her twin sister Olivia, residing in Melbourne, over 900 kilometers away, was gripped by the same inexplicable fear and anxiety.

Without understanding why, both sisters felt an irresistible urge to drive. They got into their cars and began heading out of their respective cities, drawn by an invisible force they couldn't explain. As they drove, the panic subsided, replaced by a sense of urgent purpose.

After several hours of driving, Emma and Olivia found themselves converging on a remote stretch of highway halfway between their homes. As they approached each other, they spotted a overturned car off the road. Inside was a severely injured man, trapped and in desperate need of help.

Together, the sisters managed to free the man from the wreckage and provide first aid. Their combined presence proved crucial – Emma had recently completed a first aid course, while Olivia had the physical strength needed to help move debris. The man survived thanks to their timely intervention.

When paramedics finally arrived, they stated that without the twins' help, the accident victim would likely not have survived. The remote location meant that it could have been hours before another traveler discovered the crash.

News of this extraordinary rescue quickly spread, capturing the attention of researchers interested in twin psychology and parapsychology. The case presented a compelling example of what some called "twin telepathy" – the idea that twins can share thoughts or feelings.

Skeptics argued that it was merely a remarkable coincidence, pointing out that many twins report similar experiences that can't be verified. However, the precise timing and the life-saving outcome made this case particularly hard to dismiss.

For Emma and Olivia, the experience deepened their already close bond and left them with a profound sense of purpose. They became advocates for twin research and the exploration of intuitive connections between siblings.

This astonishing tale of the telepathic twins' rescue serves as a powerful reminder of the mysteries that still surround human consciousness and the bonds between twins. It challenges our understanding of coincidence and intuition, suggesting that there may be connections between individuals that science has yet to fully explain or understand.

Chapter Ninety-Nine

The Prophetic Pottery: Ancient Ceramic Tells Modern Tale

In 1992, the archaeological community was shaken by a discovery that seemed to defy the laws of time and history. Dr. Elena Kostopolous, a respected archaeologist working on a dig site near Athens, Greece, unearthed a pottery shard that would become the center of an extraordinary mystery.

The shard, initially unremarkable among the many artifacts found at the site, caught Dr. Kostopolous' attention due to its unusual inscriptions. As she began to clean and examine the piece, she realized that the writing was in an ancient Greek dialect. However, the content of the inscription was what truly astounded her.

When translated, the text appeared to describe events from the modern era, including details of technological advancements, political events, and even specific details about Dr. Kostopolous' own life. It mentioned her by name, described her appearance, and even referenced the exact date she would find the shard.

Stunned by this impossibility, Dr. Kostopolous initially kept the discovery to herself, fearing ridicule from her colleagues. However, as she continued to verify the translation and the authenticity of the artifact, she realized the importance of sharing this find with the scientific community.

201

Carbon dating and other authentication techniques confirmed that the pottery shard was indeed from the 5th century BCE, consistent with other artifacts found at the site. This ruled out the possibility of a modern hoax. The clay, pigments, and wear patterns all pointed to its ancient origin.

As news of the prophetic pottery spread, it sparked intense debate and speculation in archaeological and historical circles. Some suggested it was evidence of time travel or ancient divination abilities. Others proposed theories about cyclical time or the non-linear nature of temporal existence.

Skeptics argued for more mundane explanations, such as an elaborate hoax that had somehow fooled the dating techniques, or a rare case of coincidental phrasing that only seemed prophetic when viewed through a modern lens.

For Dr. Kostopolous, the discovery was both exhilarating and unsettling. Her career became defined by this find, leading her down a path of investigating other potential cases of anachronistic artifacts and ancient predictions.

The prophetic pottery shard now resides in a special exhibit at the National Archaeological Museum in Athens, where it continues to baffle and fascinate visitors. It stands as a testament to the mysteries that still exist in our understanding of history and time.

This extraordinary artifact serves as a reminder that even in an age of scientific advancement, there are still discoveries that can shake our fundamental understanding of reality. The prophetic pottery remains one of the most enigmatic archaeological finds of the modern era, challenging our perceptions of past, present, and the very nature of time itself.

Chapter One Hundred

The Reincarnated Artist: A Prodigy's Past-Life Palette

In 2016, the art world was captivated by the emergence of an extraordinary young prodigy in a small town in southern France. Six-year-old Amélie Dubois began creating paintings that not only displayed remarkable skill for her age but also bore an uncanny resemblance to the style of a little-known 18th-century French artist, Jean-Baptiste Lefévre.

What made this case truly astonishing was not just Amélie's artistic talent, but her inexplicable knowledge of Lefévre's life and work. She could accurately describe his studio, his techniques, and even personal details of his life that were not widely known, despite having no prior exposure to this information.

Art historians and researchers were baffled as they verified the accuracy of Amélie's statements. She knew about specific paintings that had been lost to time, only to be rediscovered in private collections after she had described them in detail. Her knowledge extended to the minutiae of 18th-century French life, including details about clothing, architecture, and social customs that would be challenging for even adult historians to master.

Amélie's parents, both schoolteachers with no particular interest in art history, were at a loss to explain their daughter's abilities. They reported that she had begun talking about "her life as a painter" shortly after her third birthday, initially dismissing it as childish fantasy.

As news of this prodigy spread, researchers in the fields of psychology, neuroscience, and parapsychology flocked to study Amélie. Some proposed theories of genetic memory, suggesting that somehow, memories or skills could be passed down through generations. Others saw it as compelling evidence for reincarnation.

Skeptics argued for more mundane explanations, such as an elaborate hoax or an extreme case of cryptomnesia – the emergence of memories acquired in ways the individual cannot recall. However, the depth and accuracy of Amélie's knowledge, coupled with her artistic skills, made these explanations seem inadequate.

The art world was both fascinated and divided by Amélie's case. Her paintings, which seamlessly blended the style of Lefévre with contemporary subjects, became highly sought after. Museums organized exhibitions pairing her work with that of Lefévre, drawing huge crowds and sparking discussions about the nature of artistic genius and the possibility of reincarnated talent.

For Amélie herself, the experience was often overwhelming. As she grew older, she expressed a desire to develop her own artistic style while still feeling a deep connection to her "past life" as Lefévre. Her case became a cornerstone in debates about consciousness, the nature of talent, and the potential for past-life memories.

This extraordinary tale of the reincarnated artist continues to challenge our understanding of human consciousness and artistic ability. It serves as a reminder of the mysteries that still surround the nature of talent, memory, and the possible connections between past and present. Amélie's story remains one of the most compelling cases in the study of prodigies and reincarnation, inviting us to question the boundaries of human potential and the enigmatic nature of artistic genius.

Thanks for Reading

We hope you have enjoyed this book and that you will consider leaving a review on Amazon.

How to Leave a Review

1. **Visit this page: https://mybook.to/100coincidences**

2. **Scroll down to the"Customer Reviews" section.**

3. **Click "Write a customer review" and share your thoughts.**

Thank you once again for being a part of this journey.

Your support means a lot to us.

Many thanks

Copper Moom Press

Printed in Great Britain
by Amazon

53128005R00119